THE FIDDLEBACK

THE FIDDLEBACK
Lore of the Linecamp

Owen Ulph

Dream Garden Press Salt Lake City
1981

Interior illustrations are renderings of Dane Coolidge's photographs by T. Pat Leary.

Cover painting by Elna Biorge.

 Published in the United States by Dream Garden Press.

Certain passages in this book first appeared in American West and American Heritage magazines.

ISBN 0-9604402-5-9

First Edition

A limited hardbound and a trade hardbound edition have been issued simultaneously.

CONTENTS

DEDICATION

In keeping with subsequent non-conformities, I am making use of an inane rite by discharging a debt to the characters in this book whose identities I have appropriated without their knowledge. *I am rendering you crazy bastards immortal!* Hasta la vista.

Coyotin' Round the Rim...

. . . or trying to sniff out a spot to bed down in country infested with rocks, pot-holes, cactus clumps, snakes and scorpions. Most human predicaments are consequences of flaws in one's own character. However, like the Myrmidons of Achilles, well-weathered cowhands understood character flaws not as sins or transgressions of customary morality but as qualities that defined the man, neutral qualities under normal conditions yet capable of bringing fame or ruin when summoned into action in crucial situations. By urban standards, normal life in and around the linecamp could be considered a prolonged crucial situation in which ordinary time-servers who might prosper in business or politics would succumb as quickly and ignominiously as a fly unadvisedly immersing itself in a skillet of hot grease.

Ed Fisher, erstwhile cowboss of the Fiddleback, used to call me "one of them fellers who'd cut the deck below the botton card if he could slip his fingers under it." Stripped of a context, the description was neither flattering nor particularly insulting. It meant someone with the habit of explaining more than was generally necessary. According to the code of the saddle a hand should exercise restraint when offering explanations. Too often explanations had an insidious tendency to become thinly disguised alibis and a "medicine tongue" was a suspicious trait frequently betraying an uneasy conscience. "A squeaky rig can give the night-rider away," Nevertheless, while admitting a modest degree of guilt-as-charged, I plead mitigating circumstances.

First of all, this is not the book initially planned as my introduction to the authentic world of cowboys actually dedicated to working cattle. That equine masterpiece, *The Leather Throne*, begun over thirty years ago and designed to render author, cast and a singular calibre of life immortal, will, if we ever bring it under fence, speak for itself without need of prefatory comment. In the meantime, as Emma Rogers, owner, operator and oracle of the Fiddleback used to bark at my enthusiastic offers to undertake any ranch mission that provided an excuse to saddle up, "You'll be all day ketching your horse, take the pick-up." In keeping with Emma's mundane advice, I am loose-herding the following bunch of strays to the shipping pens and giving them their own road brand to pass inspection.

Secondly, this book is not directed to individuals likely to be familiar with the extinct society depicted herein, most of whom are either dead and indifferent to explanations, or have enough age on them to spin their own while they wear callouses on their elbows in the Tonapah Club, Carver's Red-Eye Saloon having long since become a trucker's stop. For the most part, this collection is directed to nostalgic contemporaries to whom the code of the saddle (not to be confused with the theatrical code of the west) would probably remain obscure without a temperate amount of explication. Therefore a sparse scattering of footnotes serving as signposts for persons sufficiently curious to explore side-trails have been shoved out of sight in an independent essay at the end of the book. This stratagem avoids the disturbing inconvenience of interrupting the sequence of the text — which the participants in the action interrupt with excessive laxity on their own. No advice, of course, is implied here. Readers are free to use the "documentation" any damned way they please.

And speaking of readers, enterprising ones, like top hands eager to get the bunch moving without unnecessary fanfare, tend to be impatient with prefaces and are likely to ride around them as if they were skirting a dead cow. Nowadays, enterprising readers are almost as scarce as top hands and the uninformed novices who might profit from reasonable guidance resist it in their hurry to satisfy a toxemic lust for vicarious sex and violence. Writers anxious to tap this lucrative, septic market are inclined to pander to the depraved tastes of their quarry instead of making impracticable demands upon sluggish intellects. Nevertheless, it will pay to read the rest of this particular preface (which is what it really is) if only to head off erroneous expectations at the pass. It is usually considered unwise to set out deliberately on unknown trails even though unknown trails often cover more interesting terrain than those well-blazed and well-worn.

ii

One of the many skills of a top hand is the ability to improvise. Jean Daniels always carried a sixty-foot reata which he had braided himself from strips of home-cured rawhide. How Jean had acquired this custom remains a mystery along with the origins of many of his unique habits and attitudes because to the best of the knowledge of anyone in the outfit Jean had never lived anywhere outside of Smoky Valley. Ed Fisher possessed the same talent, having picked it up from fire-eating *vaqueros* in Arizona where he had served his apprenticeship. Ed used his suicidal sixty feet of tensile thong interchangeably with the conventional thirty-foot hemp rope, depending upon conditions, circumstance or plain mood. Jean, however, swore by his reata and would use nothing else whether he was up-ending a bunch-quitting steer or hanging out his laundry. Cowhands, as well as Apaches, are cognizant of the remarkable properties of rawhide and the practical and sinister uses to which it can be put. Consequently, we were receptive and unsuspecting when Jean set the remains of his boiled beef and spuds on the ground for old Rex-dog to wolf down before you could begin to count his gulps and began to tell us of an occasion he pulled Luther Darrough's tractor out of an irrigation ditch where our neighborly brand inspector had thoroughly mired it trying to clean out a dam without going to the trouble of shutting down his water. Jean explained how he had soaked his reata after hitching one end to the tractor's drawbar. He'd had to unbolt the ditcher - not to lessen the weight but because the blade had dug deeply into the bank and was acting as an anchor irksome to the smoothness of the operation. He looped the other end around the base of a cedar (which later in his account he transformed into a juniper in deference to an objection that cedars were not to be found on the valley side of the highway) and then took a nap in the tree's benevolent shade. When he woke up the contraction of the sun-dried rawhide had extracted the tractor from the mud as neatly as Doc Joy could remove an impacted wisdom tooth.

All of us - with the exception of Holly Richardson, expressed genteel skepticism. Henry Steen objected that if it were that simple, we'd all be carrying reatas and having a hell of an easier job pulling fornicating cows out of fornicating bog-holes.

"I've tried that," Jean countered, stroking his gray stubble, "but it ain't often it'll work. Mostly because trees don't grow near bog-holes. You got to have something solid to hitch to. By the time you've backed far enough away from spongy ground, your reata's too short. Maybe if you was to braid yourself a specially long stretch of leather just for that purpose . . ."

Zane Hyatt got up and roughly threw a chunk of wood on the fire, setting off a splutter of sparks that made old Rex-dog abandon his tranquil wallow and retreat into the sagebrush.

"There ain't no trees near Darrough's meadows," Zane asserted brusquely," and his whole spread sprouts so many hot springs a heron couldn't find footing."

"You're forgetin' that lone juniper a-growing on the high side of his settling pond," Jean replied placidly, "that there ragged spook that keeps appearing and disappearing agin' the skyline when your riding out on the flat. Reminds me of a squatter waiting to plug you in the back if you was so careless as to come within shot-gun range."

This facile embellishment didn't appease his critics and Henry resumed his strategy of reducing Jean's anecdote to absurdity. "The only tree you'd need is the tree cinched to your roping horse," he insisted. "If he's stout enough to brace agin' a four-year old steer, he'd be stout enough to brace agin' the shrink of the reata."

"Nope! That don't work either," Jean declared. "Without a rider aboard to ease out slack, the stoutest horse ain't a-going to hold dirt against a four-year old critter thrashing about while he's being tugged ashore. And no cowhand, including Holly here, is going to be so bull-headed as to broil hisself in the hot sun a-waiting fer that rawhide to dry. An the horse ain't neither!"

"Depends on how well you've trained your horse," Clarence Genevo interjected. "I had a little blood-bay bangtail that I could leave with the reins dangling and she'd stay until her hoof took root if I didn't come back to crank her up."

Nobody was prepared to contradict this statement because except for Ed Fisher, Genevo was without peers when it came to breaking and training stock-horses. He affected a gruff manner when handling them, but they were wise to his bluff. In the training corral, they would contrive outlandish and comical antics to confound him, but once out where serious work was to be done, all nonsense vanished. I can't recall ever seeing even a green bronc buck with him. Anyway, the momentary subdued silence following his solemn assertion afforded him the few opportune seconds to saddle an elongated concoction of his own.

"One spring before Roosevelt wrecked the country I come to this chirping little stream. The kind you get to thinking about when you're pounding the drags across alkali in mid-August." Genevo explained. "I decided to let the leather cool a spell while I ketched me a mess of fresh trout. After a week or two jerky don't get much of a welcome from a hand's stomach and where I was headed I figured I'd be making a dry camp. Well, it turned out them trout wouldn't bite at nothing I'd offer 'em so I got to drifting down stream looking for a spot where I might have better luck. Any fisherman knows how that works out. I kept drifting further and further downstream fighting brush that got thicker as I dropped altitude, sampling every inviting hole and allowing time too much head. The brush finally thun out and I broke into a little pint-sized meadow as dainty as a lady's underthings—"

"When did you ever set eyes on a woman's underpants, Clarence?" Zane jeered.

"In a Sear's calalog. Where else?" Henry interceded.

Genevo ignored the obvious interruption. "It looked a likely spot for quiet casting. There weren't nothing to snag the hook nor snarl your line except a scatter of willers and a few low-growing rocks. A hand that couldn't dodge them would tangle hisself in his own loop. About then I noticed I was throwing a shadow that would have been three lengths taller than I was if you stood it on end, and I was a long way from where I'd left Hedy switching her tail and flicking her ears—"

"Hedy!" Henry scoffed. "That's a hell of a name for a horse. What was he, knot-headed, jug-headed, hammer-headed - or just headed for the chicken-yard?"

"The only critter I ever run acrosst that fits that handbill wasn't a horse," Genevo replied pointedly.

Zane vented a muted guffaw. "Any prissy puncher who calls his horse Kewpie should stay under cover."

Before Henry could muster his defenses, Genevo cut back in. "Hedy wasn't a *he*. She was a fine-limbed young mare and there was nothing wrong up here." He tapped the warped rim of his weather-stained stetson. "I named her after a movie star she reminded me of. Anyway," he resumed, returning to the main trail, "I tried a few tempting holes, but didn't rouse the appetites of nothin' but skeeters. So I chucked the pole away and started back—"

"You should of fished the riffles. Them tempting holes is strictly for suckers. Both kinds. Them in the water and them on the bank."

Genevo disregarded Zane's expertise as an angler. "Like I said, in a couple of hours it would be damn near dark. It was time to mosey along. I was still figuring to pitch camp the other side of Razorback. I wasn't eager to split that brush again and after giving the country a quick gander, I decided to fog it along the canyon wall where except for a couple of shallow side-washes choked with stunted quakers, it was pretty much open. While I was out-scrambling the lizzards, the heel of one of my boots come loose of a sudden and down I went a-bouncing like a boulder that busted off the rim-rock. When I took inventory I had me a handsome spread of assorted cuts and bruises and an ankle that had cracked apart when that no-good heel tripped me up. My war-bonnet was up in the rocks someplace."

Clarence dug into the pocket of his levi-jacket for his Bull Durham. After pouring a small mound of parched tobacco into his wisp of wheat-straw, he passed the sack around and began to build himself a smoke. Clarence was a craftsman at rolling his own and the task did not require the punctilious care and concentration he was giving it. I suspected him either of attempting to bait his audience or stalling while he contrived twists to an impromptu yarn he had undertaken with distinct knowledge of his destination, but no notion of the route he intended to take to get there. My suspicions were soon born out on both counts.

Holly, who possessed the devout innocence and ardent credibility of a child stringing beads and who, as a blithe uncorrupted spirit free from the nicotine habit, had no neurotic preoccupation to distract him from the innocuous pursuit of trouble, was the first to succumb to Genevo's shameless ploy. "What in hell did you do?" he asked guilessly.

"He died up there," Zane growled in disgust.

Genevo released a condescending chuckle. "The idea that the Devil had marked me for his beef-cut sure crossed my mind," he admitted with enough casualness to sound convincing. "I was afoot—one-footed at that—and bare-headed! I couldn't have been worse off with a twitch on me. I was plumb regretful for having trained that horse so good. If she'd been the untutored jug-head our rover boy was making her out to be, she'd of gotten impatient right quick and lit a shuck for home. When she drifted up to the corral gate and nickered loud fer grain, someone would have seen that empty saddle and savvied that something was wrong and come a-hunting me. But that weren't about to happen. Not after the job I done on Hedy."

Clarence assumed a reflective mood. The glow from the campfire and the soft sounds of the night were properly primed for it. "You know," he said, allowing his voice to subside into a drawl, "when a hand gets the feeling he's about to cash in his chips - it's happened to me a couple of times - it ain't his mother or his past sins that come to mind, it's his virtues. He regrets having had so damn many."

"I wouldn't know about that," Jean responded, always receptive to an opportunity for speculative philosophizing provided the subject did not become too ethereal or abstract, "never having run a high tally on godly qualities. But about your having done too good a job on that there horse, I'm thinking it wouldn't have made any difference over the stretch." He pawed and poked the embers of the fire delicately. "If you hadn't learned her to stay put with the reins dropped, you're enough of a hand to have staked her out solid. Even a locoed hunter can tie a horse so it don't wander off - although they seldom do it right. There was a feller come by here one time - just up there behind camp at the head of Roger's Crick - he was so a-feared his horse would get away he'd hobbled the front feet and double-tied him to a tree using both reins and a neckrope. The mahoganies was too thick to ride through so he left him there and took off chasing what he figured was a deer. A few days later a couple of Hip-O punchers, Rusty Key and Johnny-Joe Nighthawk found him sleep-walking up Indian Valley. He was as flusterated as a leppy dropped from the bunch. He'd lost his gun and couldn't remember which side of the Toiyabes he'd been on when he deserted his horse. The way Rusty tells it, the feller couldn't even remember having had a horse. I come on the carcass by accident the following spring packing blocks up to them salting grounds the Forest Service has hid away where neither man nor beast can find 'em without a topog map and a compass. That there feller was already lost when he tied up that horse. Hell, he couldn't have found his way out of a shit-wagon with the side-boards down. Hadn't even knowed how to build a bowline. Used a slip-knot and it was plain that with them hobbles hooked around its hocks the horse had fell over trying to pull loose and strangled itself. It give me the scours to see how the poor sonofabitch had scuffed up the sod fightin' to get free. If I ever meet up with the green-livered, slop-brained pig-fucker, I'd sure cotton to a chance to dish him out a mess of his own rank fodder."

A croaking chorus of assent accompanied by a sequence of gutteral epithets singled out urban nimrods both individually and as a class as sub-human entities to be despised. Even Zane, who usually defended every conventional form of masculine idiocy, conceded that the best that could be said for "them hunters that swarm from town is that as often times as not they shoot each other," to which Henry appended, "whenever dear-season comes around I slap a pair of antlers on my head to make sure I don't get shot." This tangent of discourse was given fresh deflection by Genevo directing his attention toward Jean.

"When you brung up that matter of the way Buckhouse instructs us where to plant salt reminds me of the time me and Pat O'Neil—"

"Hold that jerk-line," Holly objected, surmounting his normal indifference to procedural vigilance. "You ain't told us yet how you got out of that fix you was in."

"He never got out of it," Henry reminded Holly. "Zane told you. Clarence swapped his saddle for the halo St. Peter owed him for all them virtues and Hedy-gal is still a-waiting at the altar."

"I wouldn't put money on me being in line for no halo," Genevo replied. "When I got around to making a range count I didn't locate all the virtues I'd thought I'd put my brand on. But the few combings I ended up with, I reckon I could have lived without. I already had my ticket to Hell. Might as well be hanged fer rustling the whole herd as fer butchering a lone steer as Pat O'Neil would say.

"What were they," Henry asked.

"What were what?"

"Them few virtues you could of done without."

"Some other time," Genevo muttered. "Anyway, I knew things weren't shaping up to my liking on that plumb inhospitable mountain. It was coming on dark and I was stranded where not even a whiskey-logged hunter was about to crowd me accidentally or on purpose—"

"If I got to take any more of Clarence's tear-squeezing, I got to have a shot of jamoka to keep me awake," Jean interrupted. "Doc, you been uncommon quiet. Why don't you wrangle the pot? The cow-chips oughta have settled down by now."

"Yeah," Zane pitched in. "And be damn careful how you pour it."

I hoisted myself into action while Genevo, undismayed by apparent audience apathy, continued with his doleful memorabilia. "The cuts and bruises I could have handled, but that busted hock was determined I wouldn't make it back up that canyon. It was screaming at me through the boot leather. I'd sat there pouring sympathy on myself too long and now the boot wouldn't come off for the swelling, so I had to take my knife and slash the shank. I hated to do it because I was sportin' a right fancy pair of stompers. Even cutting 'em made me feel like I'd stepped barefoot into a bobcat's mouth. The knife was dulled from whittling that worthless fishing pole. Lucky that top-grain leather was as soft as doeskin—"

At the mention of doeskin Zane interjected explosively, "By jesus, Clarence, you've side-tracked all of us and allowed that goddam Daniels to slip off the hook - just when we'd throwed down on him and had him gut-crawling."

"The day you throw down on somebody is the day I'll build you a cold-storage box gratis," Jean remarked.

"Crawling!" Genevo echoed vehemently. "Don't never say that word in my presence - even when I'm asleep. Crawling is what I got a bellyful of that night. And when I say belly, that's only the underside of it. There's a pack-train of ways for a man to crawl that most folk never suspected - and I tried 'em all. You can locomote on your belly all right. That's what you'd think would be the easy way. But what's easy to start with don't stay easy very long. An overdose of Emma's custard or Jean's larrupin' dough gods could wear down a hand. Even a young bull can lose interest with too many heifers to take care of—"

"I don't agree with you there," Henry started to object.

Genevo cut him short. "Only because you ain't yet had time to get your fill of it!" He snorted, shook his head as if non-plussed by the congenital folly of the human species, coughed and proceeded.

"Hercules—" I began.

"Hercules be damned!" Clarence snorted. I had intended to side with him by pointing out that classical references confirmed his last example by construing the strenuous service to which he had alluded as a 'labor'. His indifference to my proferred support was mildly humiliating. From now on he was on his own. Later it occurred to me that Clarence had been thinking of a Fiddleback bull I had christened and not the Hellenic demi-god. It was my fault for having used the debased form of the hero's name. But while I was cogitating sulkily, Genevo was fully immersed in the account of his own ordeal.

"I crawled a mile down that canyon. I figured it would be worse trying to get back to my horse and climb aboard. It was my stirrup foot that was broke. Course I could have mounted Hedy from either side. That horse was a doll. Henry's name Kewpie would of fit her snug— But I'm drifting off point. Working down canyon I'd have gravity on my side. And speaking of sides, that's the first switch you make. Talk about a man crawling on his belly is nonsense. Your belly ain't built fer crawling - especially for inching over rocks. Now if you was constructed like a snake - but we ain't - at least, anatomically, we ain't. Anyway - what you do is edge over onto your side and try that for a while. You got to always use the same side because you can't drag that game leg over rough ground and you can't keep flagging the air with it from a prostate *(sic)* position. It throbs like a dying trout. You got to rest that bum foot agin' the good leg. That way you can side-wind along using your hands as levers to raise your shoulders up. Of course, I'd left my goddam gloves in the pocket of my sheepskin laced behind the cantle on my saddle—"

The horses suddenly let out a series of hysterical nickerings in the lower meadow and the sound of frenzied galloping echoed through the darkness.

"Sump'n spooked 'em," Holly said.

"An owl farted," Jean suggested.

"Just so the bastards don't romp over my bed-roll," Zane remarked.

"You call that fancy baby-blue hen-skin that looks like it's been varnished a bed-roll?" Henry asked with pointed sarcasm.

"Speaking of hosses stomping over bed-rolls," Jean commented, "there was a time up at the old Y-Bench the cavvy took offense at the night-wrangler and turned us all into sage-hens — how's that pot holding up?"

"It don't take many yards to wear out a side," Genevo seized the advantage provided by Jean's carelessly-timed request. "As you ease more and more onto your back, pretty soon you've hoisted yourself onto your butt and started to hunch along. When this gets tiresome you manage to get yourself upright and try hopping on one foot. That works for the level places, but it's no good over a rock-slide and that's about all there is along that canyon wall. So you drop back to the butt-shuffle - like you was shifting from one chair to another - except some of them talus chairs are ten feet high."

Clarence sighed from pain and exertion. "Finally, when I reached that little park where I'd wasted so much time fishing, I found me a thick, dried willer stick I could use for a crutch. Green ones got too much give to 'em—"

"For christ-sakes, Clarence," Zane expostulated, "I can't stomach any more of this crap! There ain't one of us who doesn't know what its like trying to get around half crippled up and no wheel chairs to rent. If we got to listen to bullshit, let's get back to the horse-shit Jean was feeding us—"

"I've always wondered about the difference between bullshit and horseshit," Henry commented introducing further divergencies into the course of speculation.

"Step in a pile and you'll know quick enough," Zane snapped.

"That ain't what I meant. What I'm getting at, we use them words all the time no matter what we're talking about - like riding with a loose cinch. Speaking for myself, when I say 'bullshit' I'm a mite more pissed off than if I say 'horseshit'. But Zane here switches from one to the other as carelessly as he switches brands of beer."

"You've answered your own question," I pointed out responding to my own compulsion for clarity and precision. "You imply a gradation in degree. It seems apparent that the term 'bullshit' conveys certain distinctive qualities that 'horseshit' lacks—"

"Suffering, simpering Jesus—" Jean exclaimed. (My intended treatise died in its attempt to escape from my throat.) "Whatever brand of shit you smart-assed youngsters been accusing me of dishing out just goes to show you weren't listening too close. I never held with miracles. Ain't never worked none nor knowed nobody who did. All I claimed - and still claim - is that no horse was going to stand still waiting for a wet reata to dry - especially with no one aboard to calm him down when he grew restless - and I don't make no allowances fer how well he was trained! Then Genevo busts in on me—"

"I weren't aiming to sit quiet when I knowed a horse that would," Genevo proclaimed for the second time.

"We're just going around in circles," I objected. "If we could stay on one point log enough to get a single lone critter into the chute—"

Jean shook his head with solemn gravity. "What one horse can do some of the time don't set the rules for horses of the stripe us common hands has to ride the rest of the times. And if Doc wants to make a point of staying on the point, that's exackly the point I been making all along, whether we're talking about rawhide, horses or people. What works in one case won't always work in another. Things has got to be right. That time I got Luther's tractor out of the mud all sorts of things could have gone wrong. If it had been pouring down rain, a hand couldn't have used that trick a-tall. The reata would of refused to dry. And if the sun was blistering the hide off everything as usual and that there tree hadn't give out enough shade to keep a red ant from getting a third-degree burn, or if the green-heads had been out foraging, I wouldn't have waited around myself—"

"Them's lame excuses," Henry persisted. "You didn't have to wait around. A half-mile up toward Broad Canyon, there's juniper and cedar spread out like beach umbrellas."

Jean laughed. "You ain't ketching me overheating myself hoofing it over half the continent hunting a plot of shade that's less than I kin git from my own hat. Look what happened to Clarence. A hand that lets himself get separated from his horse on purpose ought to be playing with spools."

You got me there, Jean," Henry admitted, "but now you're making out like Clarence was playing draw-poker with his eyes shut—"

"I ain't criticising Genevo," Jean said. "No doubt he'd done a top job training his horse, but a cayuse is a cayuse and no man is god. A hand who flirts with chance may not be asking fer trouble, but he sure as hell has no cause fer complaint if it smokes him out. You don't hang a man's character for gambling - only for whimpering when he loses his tail-feathers.

"I'm with Jean all the way on that," Genevo agreed, "but I wasn't gambling. I knew Hedy would be there when I come back. I just never got back."

"I wish all you fellers would tighten the latigos on your chins so Genevo could tell us how he come out," Holly complained again. "Last I remember he was limping down the crick with a busted leg."

"There ain't much use lingering over the facts till Hell secedes from Texas," Genevo conceded. "We'll shrink the rest of it the way Jean shrunk his reata. Well, I got me down there to Stone House where I knew there'd be a fair chance someone without reservations would happen along. It was a sight easier when I hit the trail that come down off the south ridge. I had to lay out that night though without even a greaser's supper. When I got to Stone House there was grub in the cellar. Since you fellers didn't show no signs of grief over the misery I suffered groping down that canyon, I'll spare you an account of the trouble I had getting through the trapdoor and down that ladder, locating canned stuff in the dark and getting back up with it. On the first ascent I'd brung up some goddam cans of green okry and had to go back down to try my luck again at finding something fit to eat. I had to wait another whole day before Billy Jim, the injun that rides for Davy Stevens, showed up a-hunting Diamond Hook strays. I'd seen a bunch holed up at the head of North Twin. He was plumb grateful because it saved him a lot of rough tracking. He went after my filly and found her right where I told him she'd be. She'd grazed a circle round herself about the size of the bald spot ringing an ant-hill. He'd seen where she trailed the few yards to water, but she'd come right back where I'd left her with the reins dropped—"

"That's the biggest load of bullshit I ever heard tell," Zane protested with exaggerated indignation.

"Horseshit," Henry corrected.

"I don't know which of you two old bastards is the biggest liar," Zane continued manifesting no inclination to recognize or argue Henry's subtle distinction. "If I was in the judge's stand I'd blow the whistle and declare 'no contest'. I'd let you fight over the purse."

"Goat-pussy!" Henry blurted the personal epithet he reserved for situations in which he wished to register his most profound and bitter scorn. "I wouldn't award no purse to neither of 'em. That there yarn of Jean's has been et raw by shirt-rats. Come to think of it I've heard it somewheres before. Only instead of a tractor, it was a loaded hay-wagon and the reata that had been looped around the axle busted and whiplashed back so hard it killed both horse and rider."

"That happened at the old Y-Bench," Jean explained with unruffled dignity. "I was there. It was my reata that broke. I could have been the one killed. That was what started me braiding my own. The way it happened was they'd unhitched the mules. Rosenkranz and Guildenstein was their baptismal names, but everyone called them Rosy and Gildy. They was a fine, stout pair and I had no trouble pulling them out. This give Jack Chatovich, who was cowboss at the time, the idea of using my reata to drag out the wagon. It also give me the idea I used later for raising Luther's John Deere. But up there no trees was near enough to hook to so they used one of the heavy team mules that out-weighed the little roan I was forking by three hundred pounds. For added ballast, they put Chub Clancey on the mule. Chub was a real hay-burner. He'd wintered extra well and was packing more tallow than three ordinary hands lashed together and loaded with Wiggins' lead doughnuts."

Jean rubbed his gray stubble over the back of his gnarled hand and went through the motions of ransacking his memory trunk. "Well, as Henry pointed out, it didn't work out like they all figured - except Henry didn't hear the story right. It's the average public that's the habitual liars, not us soured old moss-horns that's been around so long we've seen things so hard to believe it ain't necessary to make 'em up. No-account folk who ain't seen nothin' gets the habit of stitching lace on the burlap and adding frills where it ain't necessary. What happened up there at the Y-Bench was that the reata, like Henry said, recoiled when she snapped and caught that unlucky mule across both eyes like it had been cut deliberately by a spangled spic wielding a bull-whip. Naturally, that mule hauled all hell out of his shuck, windmilled backwards and landed on Chub like a hammer crashing down on an anvil. All Chub's lard never helped him none. That apple-horn gored him good. If it had been a dinner plate, he might have lived. He died four days later a-groanin' like a rusty winch. He'd made everyone so uncomfortable with his hollerin' and bellerin' all night that several of them Y-Bench punchers were for burying him the second day. But Jack Chatovich, as you boys all know, was lily-pure white and wouldn't go for it. 'You shoot a crippled hoss, but you let a man buck-out on his own,' was the way he put it, if I ain't disremembering. Rosy wasn't killed, but was blind the rest of his life. He had a prince of a team-mate in Gildy and the pair turned in some fine working years together. But when Gildy up and died in harness one winter, Rosy wasn't no use no more. He had to be fenced away from the barn corral where he and Gildy would stand motionless all day, head-to-tail contemplating each other's rumps.

He quit eating. Oats lost their attraction for him. He'd let you hang the feed-bag over his nose, but he'd just stand there and pretty soon you'd take it off again - the grain untouched. You couldn't keep him out to pasture. He'd just come back to the fence and sulk with his neck over the rail. Not long afterwards Jack found him stretched stiff behind the slaughter-shed with the magpies pecking hungrily at them blind eyes."

Jean's tone became somber, but it was impossible to tell where his irony ceased. "You youngsters high on ambition believe a lot of sweet-scented hogwash and scoff at what don't fit your fancy. Genevo's story could be true even if he sewed a few conchas onto it. True or untrue, it don't change my point none. Like I said if there was a horse that would stay put for three days without being hobbled or picketed, it don't mean it would have performed its trick that day over by Darrough's."

"I had a horse that stayed in the same place for three days," Holly testified reaching to salvage the last dregs from the pot.

"Yeah. I knew that horse," Henry said. "It was Black Susie. You let her drink bad-water when she was overheated and the reason she stayed put was she dropped dead. — For Christs' sake. Who in hell put this horse turd in the coffee?"

iii

In this instance, Henry was not indulging his appetite for exaggeration although he had not been referring to the same horse Holly had in mind. Black Suzie (there had also been a white Susie in the Fiddleback cavvy) who Holly had borrowed to ride the Shonnick on the day of her demise, had been eased into my string by means of one of those quiet collective conspiracies cowhands instinctively know when and how to bring off - another example of their talent for improvisation which, in case you have lost the wagon, is the central theme of this preface. Despite its deviousness, I intend to conclude it more or less conventionally. It should not require unusual perceptiveness to recognise that in the effort to escape the formidable literary dilemmas confronting one who aspires to write accurately, convincingly *and* engagingly about cowboys who work with cows, I may impulsively be emulating their outlandish custom of accomplishing their ends by combining homespun truth with brazen inventiveness. There are, nevertheless, limits to effective ingenuity. If the temptation to cross those limits becomes irresistible, like invading a neighboring outfit's range, I yield to it on the assumption that the strength of the impulse could only have its source in the superior veracity of myth over devitalized "facts." I am writing for neither money nor glory so there is no subversive incentive to corrupt the document. Except for purposes of an IRS classification, I am not a professional writer at all and have no inclination to become one. I am concerned only with capturing the essence of a fragment of the past that has been forfeited to mass psychoneurosis and commercialism. Ironically, I am embarrassed at producing "another book about the cowboy, God forbid!" as J. Frank Dobie decried over a half-century ago.

Since Dobie was faced with the endless stream of bucolic encyclicals he was monotonously called upon to review, there has been no let-up on the virulence of the cowboy cult. Like a plague, it has spread globally, oblivious to the excoriations of Branch, Dobie, DeVoto and a legion of sensitive critics appalled by the debasement of one of America's unique folk heroes. The phenomenon prompts a further disclaimer. It is not my objective to explode the cowboy myth by portraying him "as he really was," or to expose the horse-opera gunslinger to ridicule by contrasting him with "The Hired Man on Horseback," a hopeless cause that has already exhausted a host of zealous crusaders whose sallies Jean Daniels would have described as "barking at a knot on a fence post." Over a quarter of a century ago, Joe Frantz commented "the range rider is a myth, but nothing shall avail to cancel half a line of what the American public is pleased to believe about him." Thirty years earlier, E. Douglas Branch accused cowboy fiction of "giving the ordinary every day public what it wants, what it has always wanted and what it always will want."

I am not leaping into the saddle to stop the stampede. But I might assist in changing its direction. There are other riders on the job and they are not all just kids on horses.

In a recent commentary, William W. Savage astounded me by the degree to which he expressed my own viewpoint and seemingly anticipated the project with which I have been long engaged. "The cowboy myth is in poor condition in American popular culture," Savage wrote. "His rescue, if it is to be affected at all, must come through the efforts of intelligent people acting intelligently. Otherwise the nation stands to lose a substantial article in its cultural inventory."

One small but nevertheless important kink must be curried from Savage's statement. The cowboy myth is confused with the cowboy proper. Is the cowboy to be rescued from the cluches of the myth? Or is the myth to be rescued from the traducers who have vulgarized it?

Liberating the past from the custody of predators is a function and *duty* of legitimate historians. To accomplish this task competently and creatively requires historians with the animus of artists. Myth is more than gross fantasy and it is the discerning craftsman not the credulous idolator who sees the true light and embodies it in his work. Disciples reflect no credit on their professed masters who they exploit, despoil, embalm and preserve as bloodless ikons. Sponsors of the Cowboy Hall of Fame are likely to be irritated if not outraged by much of the content of these treatises on their enshrined relic. Likewise, western scholars who too frequently do their subjects an injustice by rendering them into dessicated abstractions, can be expected to react to the ensuing sketches with depreciated enthusiasm if, indeed, they read them at all. The subject of the cowboy, Savage states ruefully, "is so debased through commercial exploitation that people who might otherwise deal maturely with it cannot get into the mood."

Well, *I* am in the mood. As a result of dual citizenship in the academic and range fraternities (and probably more from temperament and disposition than from dubious intellectual and material influences) I am less tainted by the snobbish intellectualism traditionally directed at the low quality of western culture - real or mythical. In fact, my personal encounters with such affectation has usually been amusing. When university colleagues commiserated with me (and each other) over my degraded existence and status as a cowhand, I was tempted to plagiarize a pungent remark made by Pat O'Neil in the Tonapah jail where he was temporarily residing on a charge of non-accidental homicide. A group of us, packing smokes, sour-mash and swag from Emma's kitchen, loped into town to pay our respects and offer condolences to our fallen comrade. Pat thanked us and pointed to the stack of similar loot piled in a corner of his cell. "Say," he quipped, "you fellers are doing hard time out there."

Despite my earnest intentions, this is still "another book about the cowboy." The cynical pragmatic injunction, "if you can't beat 'em, join 'em," has always been anathema to me and I confess in advance that I am as touchy as a disturbed badger by the thought that this contribution might be so construed. At present I am convinced that I am "cutting the deck" at a reasonably proper depth. My premise, like a reliable old mustang called Come-along in whose judgment I placed confidence when I distrusted my own, is that the cowboy myth was founded upon historical reality. But that myth, born free, was soon vulgarized and fettered by a vulgarized society. Lest nervous potential readers panic and threaten to bolt, rest assured! This theme is developed in another volume "in preparation" entitled *Waiting for a Chinook* and intrudes only obliquely into the present collection which can be read for whatever amusement or informational value it may contain independent of moral or sociological significance.

Back-trailing this improvised preface (there will also be an improvised appendix) I note that it is strewn with negative contentions. Instead of hugging the timber, I'll keep in the open. Sometimes the clearest way to explain what a rangatang is, is to "tell what it ain't." Ed Fisher once sent me into Bake Oven Basin to take a "look-see" at some cows the Forest Service had reported "in trespass."

"They were ours," I announced upon return, "so I booted 'em back where they belonged."

"How'd you figure?" Ed seldom neglected the opportunity to check out the cinches on my jaw - like offering a reformed drunk the bottle to see if he'd break down and take a drink.

I'd never quite mastered the knack of reading brands and ear-marks so, after some hesitation, I blurted, "They weren't brockle-faced."

"You're improving," Ed said.

I thought his tone suspiciously casual and condescending. However, I do not wish to be accused of false modesty, but I am willing to invite the countercharge of real arrogance by promising any reader who can stay in the leather through all digressions, arcane and profane, (including the aforementioned works presumably to follow) that he will gain a thorough knowledge of cowhands and an open-range cattle operation *from the inside* without having to get his hind-end out of an overstuffed chair - and that he will add substantially to his personal "cultural inventory." If the prospect seems grim, don't buy the books. Stick to Louis L'Amour.

Cowhands, Cow Horses & Cows

In the spring of 1966, Roger Olmsted, a graphics editor of *The American West,* informed me that he had acquired a batch of old photographs of cowhorses and invited me to compose an appropriate text to accompany their publication. When the photographs arrived only one focused on a scene vaguely involving what might pass for cowhorses. In response to my lamentations, Roger replied, "Just write the damned article to fit the pictures!" The result, which you are about to read, ignited the lambent flame on the editorial board. The magazine was supported largely by respectable scholars and affluent "buffs" with a penchant for adorning their coffee-tables with *Persimmon Hill* and similarly tasteful western bric-a-brac. The single photograph capable of being contrued as representing cowhorses was of a handsome oil-painting by Olaf Wieghorst entitled, *The Lone Wrangler* and was used as the cover for the issue. The painting had to be trimmed to fit the format, but the slice left over could be viewed by opening the magazine and looking under the blanket — ideal, as a cowhand would say, "to gaze at when you're bendin' an elbow."

Unfortunately, the article itself did not quite conform to the romantic mood of Weighorst's painting. In order to check the possible mass-desertion of their subscribers, the editors engaged a retired peace-officer, W.H. Hutchinson, a fine old trouble shooter with an unblemished reputation for understanding the temperament of the real west, to introduce the essay tactfully to tender-minded readers. "This caveat," Hutch wrote, "is offered in the hope that cultists of the American West may thereby escape the thundering apoplexy induced by hearing unexpected axe blows against the bases of their most cherished totems."

Having relieved my opponents of their guns, he then gently relieved me of mine. "Astringent and impertinent, witty and wise," this graceful paladin continued, "what follows has all the pungency of a goat shed during a warm rain. And it has much more. Illumined by an abiding affection, hallmarked by a cultivated mind, it is distinguished by the ineffable qualities possible only to those who have 'laid out with the dry stock and watered from a cow track'."

Quoting this encomium in full may strike even my few votaries as shameless vanity. J. Frank Dobie cites the example of Shanghai Pierce who ordered a life-sized marble statue of himself and had it erected on a prominent knoll overlooking his Texas ranch. Asked why he did so, Pierce replied, "I knew damn well no one else would do it if I didn't!" Likewise no one is likely to pay me such extravagant tribute again and since it is too lengthy to carve on my tombstone, I include it here. Moreover, there is a more modest factor to be taken into consideration. The comparison of my deathless prose to a goat shed after a warm rain - or at any time - has all the ambivalence of one of Ed Fisher's scant compliments and I frequently take another look at the color showing in Hutchinson's pan. I always empathized with Henry Steen, who had a tough time winning at poker. You knew when he had a winning hand because he would nervously keep re-examining his hole card as if he couldn't believe his own luck. Everyone would throw in his cards and Henry wouldn't rake in enough beans to fill a thimble.

At any rate, reticence is not a quality to equip one to write effectively about the world of the cowboy. "We who knew the open range in its hey-day can be counted on one hand," Frank Harris declared over fifty years ago. "And who among that small band, except myself, is a writer of any significance?"

With characteristic western bravado, Harris cuts out a regrettable truth. Few cowhands have possessed the inclination, schooling, or talent to serve as their own press agents. In the rare instances in which they have produced them, their sketches of range life have differed significantly from the hackneyed distortions peddled by scribbling hucksters whose knowledge of the elastic market for fanciful opiates and the magnitude of human gullibility far exceeds their knowledge of cowhands, cow horses, and cows. The experience of even serious writers who have eulogized the cattle country has been, at best marginal and nostalgic. Since my purpose is to depict the cow horse and the range cow from the immediate, saddle-thumping perspective of the disabused buckaroo, a comment on the skull padding and general mental layout of this equestrian anarchist is pertinent.

Extensive contact with horses, cows and cowpokes together with the opportunity to speculate on the behavior of successful ranch owners had a corrosive effect on "character" as that sterling quality used to be explained to the errant young behind woodsheds and by an ogre brandishing a ferule in the odious offices of school principals. Why this was so should be revealed to alert readers as we traverse the rough ground ahead. A blue-ribboned specimen of the honest young puncher who underwent moral deterioration through association with the kind of two-legged and four-legged companions that are better off dead was the aforementioned Frank Harris. "Kings and cowboys I have known," he attested, "and the cowboys stand out above the rest."

Harris was not exaggerating. In the course of his life as an unsparing critic and cosmopolitan editor of a number of stylish international reviews, and as a sandhog who joined the slave-gangs who grubbed out the foundations for the Brooklyn Bridge, he had fraternized with nobility and ignobility, with the pillars of respectable society and with heretics, renegades and rebels. After an erudite and, according to Victorian standards, a salacious literary career, he pastured himself on the French Riviera and wrote *On the Trail*, a brash revelation of his early years as a cowhand. These reminiscensces astonished associates who, because Harris neither rolled his own nor hung chaps and spurs from a nail in his Mediterranean villa, had never identified him with the range. The authenticity of Harris' memoirs has been questioned by academic experts, but anyone who ever worked cattle would immediately recognize them as genuine. Harris' experiences as a cowhand account for those disreputable qualities in his writing that have been described as spurious, scurrilous, scabrous, and profane. Harris simply never shook off his trail dust. Like most well-peppered cowhands, he remained irreverent toward the values to which those raised under fence pay perfidious homage. "I have only three heroes," he boasted, "Wild Bill, Shakespeare and Cervantes — all dead." Not one of these Unholy Three was ever a cowboy, but it is not difficult to understand why they would appeal to someone with the cowboy's outlook. Harris was seventeen when he went *down* and *up* the trail in 1872. Wild Bill Hickock was at the zenith of his career and had already attained the stature of a frontier legend. Whether it was the legend of the avenging angel or the ruthless killer is not significant. All his life, Harris ignored the psalm-singers and admired individuals who got things done.

It is customary to portray cowhands as drunken hooligans contemptuous of law and order, but writers who do so are often deceived by superficialities. The film *Cowboy*, based on Harris' memoirs, showed Reece, the trail boss, splashing boisterously in his hotel tub, a bottle of booze in one hand and a six-shooter in the other, plugging cockroaches off the wall between swigs. This implausible sequence, absent from the Harris original, not only taxes credulity but also robs the cowhand's sporadic outbursts of violence and bouts with the bottle of their ethical and aesthetic components. Cowhands seldom carried shooting irons — at least during working hours. They were a handicap when riding. If one could make a "fast-draw," the weapon would certainly fall out of the holster even faster - and more often. Zane stopped carrying his after he had lost two in the sagebrush.

"They say the third time's a charm," Henry quipped, egging him on to buy and lose another. But Zane was not about to squander a month's wages again. Fortunately, for his health and future, he learned faster than he could draw.

Nevertheless, a gun was still an effective instrument of cowboy justice. Jean Daniels, a saddle-mate entitled to immortality, was once dourly watching a re-run of an ersatz western film on a television set some misguided philanthropist had rigged up in the bunkhouse under the impression that he was doing the boys a favor. The story was no worse than most such scenarios. The trail-boss hero had delivered the widow's herd to the cattle pens in Dodge City. Proceeds from the sale, of course, were to save the ranch from falling into evil hands. During the night the villain, holding the widow's mortgage, dabs the legs of the cows with boot-blacking. In the morning the local health officer pronounces the cattle contaminated with blackleg and abruptly orders the trail boss to remove the herd from town. At this point in the performance, the buckaroo audience in the bunkhouse gave vent to some distasteful utterances. But when the hero fords a shallow Malibu stream and discovers, as the boot polish washes off, that he has been tricked, Jean grimly left the room, returned with a 30.06 and, ignorant of the consequences of exploding a picture tube in a confined area, blew the TV screen to bits.

There was an interval of sepulchral silence, and then Holly Richardson, another paladin of the Fiddleback, exclaimed, "Dad-gum, Jean, that there pitcher really *did* stink." Henry Steen, in recognition of the simple heroism of the deed, performed the ultimate act of self-immolation. "I've got a quart of Jack Daniels hid in my bedroll, Jean," he announced, "and, by grab, the occasion calls for a drink!"

The shattered TV set reposed in the corner of the bunkhouse for several months before the new owner of the Fiddleback, in an initial frenzied crusade for cleanliness, order, and efficiency, had it hauled to a newly created junk yard along with tangled tons of old baling wire, a *mulada* of rusty oil drums and assorted fragments of scrap iron that would have added tone to an exhibit of modern sculpture. The cowhands worked at this assignment listlessly. As a breed, they are lean on ambition, but there is a touch of nobility to their disdain for worldly accomplishment - especially when accomplishments appear to be at odds with the humble tasks associated with daily survival. Jean, who doubled as the Fiddleback blacksmith, systematically redeemed the scrap fragment by fragment from the Sweet Dump, as it was named in honor of its creator, B.A. Sweet. While he was engaged in these salvage expeditions, Jean vigorously and constantly cursed the "waste depository" that had been bull-dozed in the undulating carpet of sage over a mile from headquarters. The pit prevented him from spotting the *right* chunk of metal needed for welding jobs that formerly he had been able to find in a few minutes scavenging around the ranch buildings.

"Cleanliness is akin to godliness, Jean," I chided him after a particularly violent outburst over failure to locate a suitable bit of angle-iron.

"God is too goddamned far away," was his curt reply. The "new owner," an ex-southern California sod-buster who had made a fortune converting a smidge of farm plot into a motel site, abandoned the Fiddleback when his three-month option expired, returned to Escondido and was later celebrated in a short paragraph in *Time* as the founder of an Anti-Tipping League. Life relapsed into normalcy at the Fiddleback and the outfit acquired a first-class sidewinder for its traditional villain and conversation-piece.

Despite tough-minded common sense and an

acute awareness of realities, the cowhand was not a utilitarian and entrepreneurial ambition seemed only another variety of visionary madness. He could not save his wages and become a cowman without losing caste. The cowman was a rancher and therefore a business man whose outlook was shaped by the balance sheet. A cowhand who found his freedom limited by concern for profit margins would have been as discomfited as a yearling with a nose full of quills. The cowhand who has the misfortune to be staked to "a little spread of his own" must eschew the nomad's way of elegant independence or go belly up. Either property or marriage, or worst of all the combination of both, was the fall into the Big Rut - and a "rut," as defined by the cowhand, was "a grave open at both ends." This tragic dilemma confronted my friend Carl V. Haas, who discovered the impossibility of reconciling liberty and honor with solvency. He chose solvency and, thereby, forfeited the privilege of playing a leading role in *The Leather Throne.* Such was the malignance of Haas' predicament, as with many modern ranchers, he was forced to corrupt himself even further by becoming a financier to secure his position as a cowman. "The drawback to succeeding as a cattleman," he complained as he watched the range secede from his life steppe by steppe, "is that a hand is forced to hang up his saddle." No cowhand in his right mind would have wanted to *own* the Fiddleback - although he was always brimming with notions on how it should be run.

While the cowhand may have had his stock of

vices, there was one virtue he could not afford to be without, and that is an elusive quality called "gumption", a topic which will probably harry you like a persistent horse-fly throughout these discourses. On the range, lack of gumption showed up like a bare-assed nigger in a snow-drift - to crib one of Henry's favorite if mildly barbarous similes. A muddling cow-hand sooner or later eliminated himself without help or hindrance from fate or his fellows. This is not to underrate the influence of chance. "Lightning can strike a virgin in church," was Jean's terse comment to Zane when this perennial candidate for catastrophe had castigated every conceivable animate and inanimate entity, with the exception of himself, for having been responsible for his nocturnal collision with a group of fornicating horses loose on the fornicating highway. If the fornicating moon had been where it fornicating well belonged "it wouldn't have happened" was his remarkable conclusion.

"You been living on extended credit ever since your old man caught your mother bent over in the barn," was Jean's caustic comment.

Since chance is something no one has ever been able to do more about than cut back on its grazing rights, there is no point in useless grousing when it drifts onto your range - which is showing gumption. Gumption lets a hand know how far he can press his luck before he can expect it to run out. When gumption finally catches up with him, he knows that luck is something that can never be crowded at all.

The *Fiddleback Almanac* maintains that luck operates in one direction—in a hand's favor. The disasters that befall him are those he probably deserves. If he is dozing when his horse steps in a badger hole and he awakens with a broken neck—he had best forget it. The "accident" was a predictable consequence of having carelessly trusted chance. But if he can climb back into the saddle, he should add to his tally of luck. The devil had just wasted a loop, but he'd sure in hell try again! This attitude shows gumption. It is the attitude of most cowhands, and it keeps them agreeable and uncomplaining. They know when they have drawn their wages in advance. They know that everyone uses up his share of celestial beneficence before leaving the weaning corral. They realize that a hand's personal appearance among the living was an improbable event in the first place. They figure they are ahead of the game just to be sitting in on it. They are content breathing fresh air or foul, owing nothing to anyone, and expecting nothing.

Gumption does not demand faked humility, but it does demand a sense of reality and a nose for smelling out humbug. A hand may figure he is "pretty hot potatoes" with a rope and may pride himself on his ability to stick to the back of anything with hair. While these are useful talents to carry in stock, they are not enough to keep him out of a pinewood box because all they require is muscle, guts and coordination. It is gumption to recollect that the scrawniest piece of buzzard bait that ever chewed hay has got a human outclassed in all these qualities. The cowhand's margin of superiority is thin. The only real edge he has over this four-footed tornado is his gumption, and he has to wear it in easy reach all the time.

ii

More nonsense has been written about the horse than has been written about any topic with the possible exception of religion and Shakespeare. While cowhands become convinced that nature designed the human hind-end for no other purpose than to occupy a time-tempered old leather hull, this attitude should not be confused with the zealotry of saddle-addled cultists. A cow-hand does not *enjoy* riding. With mild provocation, the most unimaginative ranny can become an artist at dissimulation. Rheumatic pains, or aches tracing their origin to legendary saddle injuries, have a habit of showing up in vile weather, and "roping arms" suddenly "go stiff" as the corral dust thickens during an extended *auto da fe* at branding time. In winter the hand will hug the kitchen stove stretching his mug of morning coffee to stave off saddling up as long as the patience of the cow boss will hold out. Since the cow boss is a cowhand himself, he is usually a willing accessory to the vice of "playing the pot" until he shoulders the conscience of the crew.

Stated bluntly, to the cowhand the horse is just an animated tool. Riding for any purpose unrelated to working cattle seems indecent to him, and no self-respecting hand would go near a horse in town. Strutting a pony around city streets or cantering it along an oiled bridle path protected from a hissing freeway by a twelve-foot chainlink fence would only occur to him in a nightmare. He would seldom be found in a rodeo parade if promoters did not make participation a clause of the contract permitting him to contest. Rodeo parades, according to Jean Daniels, consisting of "assorted frauds clomping along the hot pavement astride powdered palominos, followed by full-feathered mounted contingents of overfed businessmen posing as a sheriff's posse make about as fool a spectacle as grown folk kin put on."

Horse-struck characters who pay sizable sums to keep some sugar-cruncher in a swank stable impress the cowhand as being "plumb locoed." Many top hands actually hate horses—with some reason. It is not accidental that hippophilia is limited to urban cultures that have ceased to depend upon this highly unstable beast as a means of locomotion and, consequently, know very little about its perverse habits.

The truth is that horses exhibit, in an exaggerated form, many of the worst characteristics of people. They are greedy, envious, spiteful, malicious, slothful, superstitious, and stupid. They are congenital hysterics and each one is, ominously, a prospective homicide. If horses could talk, they would lie!

A well-broken horse is one in which these traits have been partially sublimated, but it is necessary to remember that they are latent and, regardless of training, the animal will always function on the brink of hysteria. This inclination to panic if a jack-rabbit springs suddenly from behind a clump of rabbit-brush is probably the paramount feature of the horse.

Hours can be spent attempting to condition him to equanimity be waving a burlap sack or saddle blanket in front of his eyes or clattering pans about his ears. Modest results are attainable if one is prepared to accept the fact that almost any unexpected or unfamiliar situation will revive the animal's inherent idiocy. A discarded bean can that a horse has not previously seen along the trail will make him balk.

It was impossible to ride Gizzard, a relatively sane old mustang, past a heap of dried-up cow bladders baking in a desert boneyard. After much snorting, head tossing and eye popping on his part, I climbed out of the saddle, dragged one of the odious relics in front of his quivering nose, but still had to lead him reluctantly forward on foot.

Holly Richardson was once descending South Twin Canyon in the moonlight when, rounding a turn in the dark trail, he suddenly found himself staring at a black, brockle-faced heifer. Shiner, a thoroughbred he was riding that should have behaved more in accordance with its aristocratic lineage, let out a screaming nicker, turned tail and bolted back up the canyon. Holly, a top hand, was unable to bring him under control until they had reached the line camp at Roger's meadow.

In defense of what appears to be excessive volatility, it should be taken into account that a horse's ability to focus his eyes is significantly different from that of a human—or from any other living creature with the possible exception of a zebra. Henry Steen, who claimed to have once ridden a zebra, insists that it is worse than a horse. "It ain't only that it can't focus right," he explained, "them zebras is all cross-eyed from looking at other zebras."

Leaving the account of Henry's encounter with zebras for some more auspicious occasion, we will return to the subject of the horse. The middle range of its vision is an optical mystery. I have endured them stubbornly loping along with me on the extreme edge of the rim-rock when they could just as easily have navigated a yard or two to the left in safety and comfort. I have had them appear to be riding hell-bent for badger holes yawning at us like a hippopotamus getting ready to hit the sack, only to have them skip crisply over it at the last fraction of a second. "All you can do is trust the sonsabitches," was Jean's lean advice in the wake of my analytical complaints.

I found his words as reassuring as to be told that the way to cure a tooth-ache is to cut off your head, but time and experience demonstrated the wisdom of the prescription. The horse's sensory equipment enables it to see, hear and smell things which to a human apparently do not exist. Consequently we cuss them out for the irritatingly idiotic habit of conjuring up phantasies and behaving as if they were real.

"I don't hold that again' 'em," Jean said. "Remember when you was a kid alone in the dark. My dad would just laugh at me and I learned not to admit I was plumb scared. I figgered if that sour old bastard had lived as long as he had doing things that'd make a grizzly think twice, I guessed I could handle a few noises I couldn't see. And that's about as much as you can learn your horse. If you're there on his back, he's going to feel a lot less like spooking than when you ain't. A horse can smell fear. If you're scared, he'll be scared. And if you're scared of him, he'll be scared of you."

Horses hate each other more than they hate cowhands. But isolate one from the bunch and if a rider is not along to quiet him, he will race up and down the fence whinnying frantically to find an opening that will let him rejoin his despised fellow jugheads. If another horse is not pastured with him and patience is not taken to tuck him into his new bedding ground, he will likely try to clear any obstruction that hinders him. If it happens to be barbed wire he will cut himself to pieces in unreasoned frenzy where a cow would calmly scrape her way through unscathed. A week later, if still alive and given the opportunity, the horse will repeat the performance. This is intelligence? Some old horses entangled in wire will stand still until a savior appears with wire cutters, but they are exceptional.

A major consequence of hysteria is that a horse, unlike a cow, is always getting hurt. Cows may be susceptible to pinkeye, blackleg, redwater, greenhoof, bluehorn and tailrot, but except for a tendency to commit suicide grazing along the highways, they are not particularly accident prone. A horse, on the contrary, is almost impossible to keep from trouble. If one were to hobble him in a living room, he would eventually gash pastern or fetlock on the hearth fender. To gamble on rearing a horse from colthood to maturity without having him permanently maim or disfigure himself is to challenge frightful odds. Horse breeders are unflagging optimists.

To watch a newly born colt frisking in the spring grass almost vindicates Disney's mawkish sensibility, and to see the flight of horses, tails bannered, galloping majestically across the unfenced sage is indeed a euphoric spectacle. But there are moments when they are rabidly raising clouds of dust and manure inside the corral, crowding, kicking, and biting each other, when one would like to exterminate the lot. At feeding time they fight greedily even when there is more than enough hay for all. No matter how many piles are scattered, each horse will want to devour every stack at once. During roundup it is necessary to tie each animal to the rail individually before putting on the nose bags, which makes feeding a time-consuming chore, especially after a hand has been pounding leather from dawn until dusk.

Barney Manor, a sentimental old hand who should have known better after sixty years of wrangling, once tried a shortcut by attempting to grain the horses without first having separated and tied them along the fence rail. We had sent him loping on ahead to rustle grub for both us and the stock so that we would not have to address ourselves to these tasks in the dark. When we returned to camp, he was stretched out serenely under the willows. We thought he had gone to sleep and were in the act of cussing him out when we saw the horses tossing a dozen mangled burlap sacks about the meadow. Jean immediately figured what had happened. Sure enough, when Barney was examined more closely his cracked skull was dunking in a pool of blood. We could not pack him out before morning, but since he kept everyone awake all night with his wretched groaning, it was evident that he would live.

The cow horse's greed for oats can produce a certain amount of low comedy. Holly Richardson once had a clumsy brute step on his foot while he was shoeing him. The foot swelled so much that Holly could not get his boot on. Determined not to be accused of goofing off, Holly wrapped his foot in burlap and tied it with baling twine. The horses took the bulky brown bandage for one of the improvised nose bags to which they were accustomed and chased him all over the meadow biting at the injured foot. In perilous predicaments of this sort, no buckaroo would consider coming to another's assistance. It would have been an insult to Holly's honor not to allow him the privilege of extricating himself from his self-created plight. While the roundup crew rollicked with laughter and offered assorted raucous advice and encouragement, Holly managed to get his knife from his pocket, cut the burlap loose and hobble barefooted to the fence, leaving the gluttonous nags to their tug-of-war with the empty sack.

Anectotes to illustrate the churlish and malevolent traits of cow horses are inexhaustible and can be curtailed, but a cursory comment on the horse's reputed intelligence is essential. While a horse is fundamentally stupid, he is not lacking in diabolical cunning. Even in humans, stupidity and cunning are frequently combined, and it is a common mistake to assume that the latter excludes the former. Intelligence is allied with ethics, and ethics is an aristocratic quality incompatible with cunning, a peasant quality. Consequently, intelligent individuals are handicapped when confronted by cunning idiots unless they recognize that the latter are not entitled to be treated as peers—as was understood in the saner days of feudal society by a ruling class whose wisdom was acquired from extensive experience with horses.

Liberalism, in short, is the first creed to be set aside when dealing with the cow horse which, by no stretch of the imagination, can be considered a noble animal because it lacks an ethical sense and operates on the lowest level of self-interest. Elsewhere, I contradict, but *do not retract,* these statements. When once accused of contradicting himself, Lenin replied, "Very well, I contradict myself." A truly great man—with gumption. History contradicts itself! One of the most cunning blackguards with whom it was my misfortune to become acquainted was a veteran Morgan whose name must be disguised in the interests of delicacy. Bomber—let us call him—never bucked in the early mornings when he was supposed to and the rider was prepared to be "shook up." He would wait until midafternoon when his rider was languishing, saddle weary, wondering if he would ever make it to the ranch with his bunch in time for the dinner gong. Bomber would pick his moment. Drop a rein and lean forward to retrieve it, or miss the stirrup when climbing into the saddle, or ride him down a precipitous slope, or try to get aboard from the downhill side, or be smothered in a thicket of "quakers" or mahoganies . . .! Bomber knew how to exploit any advantage. It was always his ambition to be ridden by a cow hand with a broken back, but no one gratified him. A horse's malicious, spiteful cunning is something always to be on guard against. A good hand can maintain supremacy by purposeful deception (called by Pavlovian psychologists "conditioned response") and the use of the opposable thumb—which the Hellene Xenophon demonstrated in a perspicacious treatise on the *Art of Equitation* almost twenty-five hundred years ago.

If the reader resents the above allegations as defamation of the character of the "noble steed," he should perform a few simple experiments. Place a new horse in a field occupied by entrenched incumbents, and the old horses will run the newcomer ragged, giving it no peace to graze and lacerating its body with their teeth and hooves. Sympathy for the victim is wasted, however, because it will, in turn, administer the same schoolboy treatment to the next novitiate introduced into the herd. Every bunch has its bully. Remove the offensive troublemaker and a new one will immediately emerge to take its place. The persecuted are always eager to become persecutors. Every horse should be branded with a swastika.

Nothing that has been said is altered by the fact that most cowhands become attached to some old horse that has served them well. This testifies only to the sentimentality of the hand and not to the nobility of the animal. When a cowhand has ridden a horse for fifteen years over every kind of terrain and in every kind of weather, when he has roped thousands of calves from him, cut and trimmed herd after herd with him, watched the ice form on his nostrils in winter and the lather bathe his hide in summer ("a busy horse is a happy horse"—a bit of ancient lore which was once applied with considerable success by parents to children), it is not strange that he should lose detachment in assessing the animal's true disposition. The days his horse hid in the buckbrush when it was needed in a hurry, the days when it broke into the barn and almost foundered itself on stolen oats, or sneaked into the hay corral, chewed the bales and demolished the stack, the several instances in which it tore loose from the hitching post, stepped on the reins and snapped them, rolled over with the saddle and busted the tree, got the bit in its teeth and bolted into the swamp carrying the cowhand with it, shook with him until his innards rattled, swept him under a mahogany limb, or caused him contusions on both knees as it plunged between a pair of close-growing quakers, stumbled with him (once in the middle of the creek), jammed him into the fence smashing a leg and a stirrup, ate his chaps, pulled its picket pin and left him stranded at line camp to hoof it to the ranch packing his gear—days which, at the moment, made the cowhand feel like pawing dust, become, with the mellowing of time, occasions for senile chuckling. But all the cowhand has to do is get back into the saddle, and the realization that the animal beneath him is an on'ry sonovabitch quickly returns. The best that can be said for the cow horse is that it is not a hypocrite and ultimately is preferable company to most humans.

iii

Cows have come off a poor third relative to the cowboy and the cow horse in the literature of the West. No one refers to this much-abused stoic as the "noble cow" or "man's best friend." The closest the cow has come to attaining stature and prestige is through the longhorn branch of the family. For the most part it has simply remained "the critter." In recent years Brahma steers have been restoring some luster to the breed, but this is more than nullified by the eradication of horns and the economic incentive to butcher every nonproducing animal by the time it reaches eighteen months, thus making cow punching a tamer craft than it was when four-year-old steers weighing in the neighborhood of fourteen hundred pounds plunged and snorted at the end of the cowhand's rope.

It is not my intent to compose an apologia for the cow which, in most respects, is far more obnoxious than the horse, but only to place the creature in proper perspective. Since, directly or indirectly, it is eventually destined for the slaughterhouse, it seems unwarranted to expect reasonable cooperation from this victim of man's carnivorousness. Consequently, the invective and infinite unsavory sobriquets and epithets hurled at the critter by buckaroos outraged by her sullen resistance to her destiny have not seemed deserved. But a cow outfit is not an arena for the enactment of justice.

If, indeed, the cow outfit serves any metaphysical purpose, it is as an enormous stage for the presentation of an unending play in which a creature of unrestricted autonomy sits on the back of a creature of feverish volatility and together they struggle to subjugate a creature whose chief characteristic is perverse intractability., So uncanny is the intuition of the cow that it can almost always sense what the rider wants it to do, and do the opposite. The cow's flaw is that it is so addicted to this course of action that a shrewd hand can turn the animal's perversity against itself.

Jean Daniels maintained with conviction that the way to induce cows to eat up old rotten hay is to fence the stack, since any obstacle designed to impede a cow's whim only invites the animal to make an assault upon it. The same fence that cannot keep a cow from the alfalfa field will effectively prevent the cowhand from driving it back out. Ranch dairy cows, despite their docility, are virtuosos at sabotage. The moment their heads are in the stanchions and the process of milking is launched, they will relieve their bladders and defecate effusively. They will wait patiently until the milking pail is full before kicking it over. This demonic behavioral pattern incited (or "inspired") Jack Chatovich's *Ode to a Sego Milk Can:*

> No tits to pull
> No tail to switch
> Just punch two holes
> In the sonovabitch.

Moving a herd of cattle across the flats against a dust-laden wind will convince a cowhand, especially if he is pounding the drags, that a cow covers a shorter distance in a longer time than any form of life that does not sink roots into the sod. No amount of shouting or baking the horse can prod the herd into increasing its pace. A temporary spurt will be offset by a later slack-off. In the mountains, however, where maneuverability is limited and the same cows have horse and rider at a disadvantage, they will exhibit unusual vitality. A small bunch of cows grazing serenely on a sage-covered slope will, on the sudden appearance of a rider, skirt the contour of the hill with unbelievable rapidity—without exceeding a trot. Humping and snorting up the slope to get above them, or crashing over rocks and brush that rake the horse's belly, it is almost impossible to outstrip the infernal critters before they slip over a ridge into an adjacent canyon or disappear into a grove of mahoganies.

One memorable February, Holly Richardson and I drove two hundred heifers from the home ranch to winter range on Miller's Flat, a distance of approximately a hundred miles. The drive took five days. We settled the herd on water, loaded our horses into a stock truck, and returned to the ranch by the highway. We were awakened the next morning by the harmonious bawling of half the herd outside the corrals. They had cut themselves out from the bunch at Miller's Flat and made the return trip in a single night. Episodes of this sort minimize a hand's sympathy for foot-sore, trail-weary animals.

If one wished to experience exasperation, frustration, and despair in a concentrated capsule, he would need only to take on the task of bringing a brush-hugging bull off summer range in the Toiyabe

National Forest. The only time I have been brought to tears since the age of seven was in the course of driving one of these bulking paragons of sullen obstinacy from the head of Reese River across the divide and down South Twin River to Smoky Valley. Thickets of willow, wild rose, elderberry, and assorted vines imported from hell were so tangled that it was impossible to figure out how any animal larger than a wood mouse could have managed to penetrate them. But this bull did—not once, but a hundred times in every agonizing mile. Gizzard, who normally took brush like a high-speed tank, was useless. It was necessary to dismount, crawl through the undergrowth on foot, and beat the four-footed bigot back onto the trail, hacking at his rump with the rowel of a hand-wielded spur. After hours of this punishment, scratched, torn, bleeding, with twigs, dry leaves, and famished spotted ticks down my back and in my boots, I threw a rope on him and dragged him down the trail an inch at a time. Don't tell me it cannot be done. It has!

In the corral, cows can be equally obtuse. They can blindly hit a stout fence as if it were a dried reed. The best corral I have ever seen was at the Campbell Ranch near McDermit. This stockade was built from railroad ties set vertically in a trench of concrete, an eight-foot and a five-foot tie alternately touching each other. The entire enclosure was further reinforced by a double, twisted, three-quarter-inch cable laced tightly across the open spaces between the tall ties and the short ones. It was an inspiring fence! But then I have not seen it since it was used to hold cows.

The best position for a cow is lying flat on its side when two good cowhands have it roped at both ends and have their ponies backing up taut in opposite directions. For extra measure, a couple of sturdy hands from the ground crew should be sitting on neck and haunch to make certain the nooses do not slip. Then a hand can roll a smoke.

A cow is a particularly ungrateful critter. Every time one is pulled from a mudhole she will take after her benefactor the moment she feels hard ground underfoot. The best policy in "bog pulling" is to choke the animal *almost* to death while extracting her. In this way the cowhand has time to remove the rope from her throat while she is still gasping and in a daze. It is a thrilling moment between the interval in which the rope has been disengaged and the hand has regained the saddle. On one dramatic occasion, a mean old sister had lodged herself helplessly in a water trough. Henry Steen gallantly placed himself in jeopardy wrestling the animal's frantically kicking legs into a position where it could obtain some semblance of Archimedean leverage, with Holly assisting from the back of his horse. Henry was lucky. His only reward was a vicious hook in the ribs and a ripped shirt. It could have been a casket.

Despite their blatant bawling and their readiness to "go on the prod" when disturbed, cows are remarkably insensitive to pain. While being unloaded, one of Carl Haas' steers caught its hoof between the rocking bed of a cattle truck and the chute. Pressed from behind by other steers and goaded by insensate teamsters stabbing it with a hot rod, it pulled its foot off. It limped down the chute into the corral and immediately began to munch hay. Even the toughest Marine will lose his appetite after an amputation without anesthetic. About an hour later the steer died, but it died on a full stomach.

Contrary to general opinion, cows do not all look alike. They possess definite individuality, in bodily contour, facial expression, and temperament. I am convinced by personal observation that Ed Fisher knew every cow in the Fiddleback herd. Moreover, he could remember animals for years back. Herds also have subtle family characteristics. Ed taught me this in a lesson that took less time than it would take to drop the handle of a hot skillet.

Cows are curious creatures, and to observe their habits closely is more informative than courses in animal psychology. On the range, cows will travel many miles to drink. A bunch will start for the water hole at the same time, stringing out across the sage in single file and rarely pausing to graze along the way. They travel solemnly, with purposeful dedication. They will leave one cow behind baby-sitting with a group of calves. When they return, the patient guardian will take her turn. If a cow is separated from her calf, cowhands do not normally interfere. Cows and calves will "mother up" unless the herd is unusually large and has been considerably smoked and riled. If a cow loses her calf along the trail, the buckaroo will cut her from the bunch. Both animals will find each other at the place of last sucking. Cows face the same direction when grazing. Horses will graze with no uniform pattern. Cows lying in the grass will suddenly get up at the same time. This phenomenon is most apparent at night. These are matters of common cow lore which, while defying rational interpretation, have inspired cowhands to spin interminable extravagant theories around many a potbellied stove and open campfire. Awkward and obstinate as the cow may be, her existence has saved both the cowhand and his cow horse from extinction. Without the blessed cow there would have been no cowboy legend and the "western tradition," forced to depend solely on pious, sod-busting dirt farmers and drunken miners who spent their sober moments down a hole, would have been deprived of most of its color.

iv

For the past century it has been customary to lament the passing of the cowboy and the free range and I am reluctant to take up the chant with the throng of mourners already attending the wake. To do so would seem to indicate lack of gumption as I have described and extolled it as a cardinal virtue. Yet one of the greatest human fears is the horror of being buried alive. When this tribute to a misrepresented sub-culture was first written, it was with the opinion that its subjects could still be found thriving with undiminished vigor in scattered sections of the Rocky Mountain states. After all, only a few years had elapsed since I had been part of it. Although Texas, Arizona and Colorado had been surrendered to the dudes, Montana, Wyoming, Nevada (excluding

Sodom and Gomorrah) and vast areas of central Canada were still cliff-hanging. Northern Mexico was a stronghold of fantastic cattle empires. The story was being told of a smug California cattle-buyer who arrogantly asked an old *ranchero* from Hermosillo if he could deliver five thousand head of two year old steers. The *ranchero* thoughtfully stroked his closely cropped, well-groomed gray beard and replied, "*Si senor. Que color?*"

This brings to mind an authentic anecdote which originated in my presence in September, 1957. Fletcher Wiley drove into Smoky Valley from Lancaster, California and addressed Carl Haas, who was then twenty-eight years old and had taken over custody of the Fiddleback from Emma Rogers and expanded the operation significantly. Fletch, in the condescending tone of baronial supremacy, asked, "Young man, can you pasture eighteen hundred head of braymer steers?" Without hesitation, Haas responded, "Old man, not only can I pasture 'em, I can hide 'em."

Haas' histrionic braggadocio is vindicated by the unrehearsed spontaneity of his humor. He possessed a natural command of traditional western wit, but he learned to suppress it in the pursuit of a career more suitable to the world of his contemporaries. Revision of these sketches has produced temporal confusion and raised difficulties in the use of tenses. I oscillate between the present and the historical past. For example, I quoted Haas as complaining that the price of becoming a modern cowman was the sacrifice of the saddle—as if the choices bore equal weight on the scales. There had been a day when such a free choice could have been exercised—when a consecrated cowhand could have continued to practice his craft and honor his code while leaving the spoils of worldly ambition to those who, while boasting of their cowboy heritage, had voluntarily abandoned it. But that day was past. Haas had no choice—at least no sane one. He simply chose survival over extinction. His ordeal described some years ago in an article entitled "The Cowboy's Lament" for *Arizona and the West* was sociological—not moral. Carl appreciated the profile except for my injudicious use of the phrase, "He could talk a gopher out of its hole." As a cowboy, he would have chuckled. As a future Cattleman of the Year and an aspiring financier, he found the phrase embarrassing. I render him my apologies. He may never have talked a gopher out of its hole, but he talked me into a lot of them.

No, Haas indeed had no choice. Nor did the men who preferred to remain cowhands. The irreversible trend toward mechanization and automation of beef-production, together with the ruthless exploitation of the "open range" by land speculation, industrial development and "defense" promotion was bringing about the extermination of the cowhand, cowhorse and even the cow in its historic role as "the critter." In the fall of 1951, the Fiddleback made its last shipment of four-year old steers. The men who worked them were all in their fifties and Emma Rogers was still the Lord of the Manor. I did not want to see these earthly giants buried alive. My association with them inspired me with a desire to document their existence in a manner of which neither fiction nor factual treatise is capable. But if that society was not dead then, it is now. Today both the cowman and the cowhands have gone. The cowman is now a farmer, an agro-industrialist or an aggregate of absentee corporate investors. The only refuge for displaced cowhands, if there are any, is in some ostracised saloon in some former cow-town now hi-jacked by the local Chamber of Commerce catering to tourists, truckers and the Highway Department. Here these casualties of Growth and the G.N.P. can exchange tall talk with other outcasts.

the Critter

It was the time we were working out of the Diamond Hook, Davy Stevens' starve-out operation at Cloverdale in northern Nevada. Cloverdale was the cluster of sod and tarpaper shanties the Fiddleback was using as a line camp late that particular fall, and Davy Stevens was the eighty-year-old cowman who held title to the spread. The Fiddleback and the Diamond Hook outfits shared a corridor of range through the San Antone sand hills, and we used to help Davy with his riding. Holly Richardson and I had cut three hundred two-year-old heifers from the Fiddleback bunch and had herded them down to

Miller's Flat where they could winter on rabbit brush, browse, and alkali. The range down that way was usually free from snow cover. They would scrounge and learn to make out.

We had dropped them, loaded our tired horses into the stock truck that had been left for us, and, with indecent haste, bumped back to Cloverdale, where we submerged ourselves in the luxury of lumpy, rat-stained mattresses in place of gravel, downy sage, and rabbit pellets.

Long before daylight had wiped out all but a couple of lingering stars, we were awakened by old Jean Daniels' gruff chuckle. (He never slept beyond 3 A.M.) "Your girls is back."

How Jean could tell the bellowing of a heifer from that of a full-grown cow was something I never figured out, but sure enough, there they were, bawling outside the west pasture fence.

Let me make the situation clear: we had all but taken root in our saddles inching those surly laggards along the dusty flat at a pace that would have made a snail impatient. Fifty frying miles. Three forty-hour days. And now in a single night the ornery brutes had retraced the full distance it had taken those three days to travel!

"You should've stayed with 'em until they was settled," Jean said.

"Kee-rist, Jean," Holly protested, "we located em on water an everything. . . ."

"You don't never trust 'em," Jean muttered, giving us the benefit of his experience. "They're *critters.*"

ii

"*Critter*" is a term seldom found in action-packed oaters in which the cowboys usually manage to avoid encountering cows. But to the hand with no time for draw-downs and shoot-outs at dawn or sunset because he had been pounding leather long before and long after these approved hours for gunplay, "critter" was an indispensable part of his working vocabulary. He did not employ the term loosely. Like all cowboy lingo, "critter" has a tightly fenced context—one of the few points that slipped the noose of Ramon Adams in his otherwise perceptive *Dictionary of the Range, Cowcamp and Trail.* Although obviously a corruption of "creature," a word referring to all God's loved ones, great or small, the cowboy restricted "critter" to the cow. "The whole bovine family," writes Will James, "whether they're papas or mamas, sons or granddaughters, all are called cows by the range rider, or critters." James illustrates the exclusive nature of the word by recounting a dispute with another line rider as to whether a speck on a distant ridge was a horse or a critter. James bet a dollar it was a critter. The object of controversy turned out to be a horse, and James lost the bet.

James deserved to lose his dollar for allowing slack to gather in his prose. "Cows" and "critters" are not synonymous terms. The former is a neutral noun, the latter packs a judgment on the animal's character. Unless the speck on the ridge was a perverse bunch-quitting stray, it could not have been a critter; it had to be a cow. Cattlemen, by which is meant bucolic capitalists, would refer to their stock as "cows," thinking of them collectively as marketable units of beef-on-the-hoof. It was only the cowboy who called cows "critters" and then only when he was dealing with them as willful entities reacting with varying degrees of obstinacy to his efforts to educate them. No cowboy would ask a rancher, "How many critters do you run?" but he could easily remark, "John Casey runs the worst bunch of critters that ever busted out of hell's corral!" Summoning Will James back to the witness stand, "The critter . . . is the mean-eyed, sharp-horned, kink-tailed animal that cowboys or any others that know her don't fall in love with. She's ungrateful, independent and ornery . . . she sure don't never show any appreciation. Just let the green grass come and see what happens. There won't be no mild nor thankful look in her eye for the hay that was handed her when the drifts was deep, and she won't beller no thanks for being pulled out of the bog she got into, instead she'll hit for the brush at round-up time and chase the cowboy back on his horse if he tries to . . . get her out."

A long list of philanthropic services rendered the ungrateful critter by the company of mounted friars who minister to her incessant needs can be added: innoculation against a plethora of potential diseases; dipping and spraying against the afflictions of flies, grubs, and assorted pests; doctoring for pinkeye, foot rot, lump-jaw, gotch ear, blue tail, bloat, red water, staggers, and spangs; pumping water during droughts, breaking ice on frozen water holes in sub-zero weather, and constructing windbreaks against northers; planting trees for back scratching, rump rubbing, and shade—all these plus a myriad of unique, nonclassifiable acts of attention such as the time Henry Steen rescued a critter that had wedged itself upside down in a trough, or the time Zane Hyatt sawed another loose from the outhouse at Cloverdale that it had no business investigating in the first place.

Despite such abundant benevolence, the cow has very little to be thankful for, and gratitude toward mankind is not a virtue one should reasonably expect it to display. Any generosity shown the cow is strictly utilitarian. Hay pitched when the drifts were deep was not forked out as an act of charity. Starved cows produce no return on investment, and all the cures inflicted without anesthetics are something the animal would willingly forgo. All the sinister grooming is directed toward ulitmate butchery. Cows instinctively know this (there is much evidence that cows possess ESP), and consequently their reluctance to co-operate in their own eventual destruction should not be regarded as an indication of defective character. "Critter," though a derogatory expression, is not entirely an epithet. The critter was the cowboy's Miltonic Satan—a salty adversary. Until this luckless victim of man's carnivorous greed was roped at both ends and pinioned by a member of the ground crew, one knee thrust against its neck, one hand gripping a foreleg and the other yanking up its snout, it was not safe to relax in the saddle and roll a smoke. Anchored to the prostrate critter and temporarily secure in his leather throne, the cowboy could reflect upon the diverse imbroglios of existence.

Pat Fee, who would haul the devil from a live volcano, skin him, and throw him back if I were to refer to her as a "cowperson," once wrote to me from her remote spread on the fringe of the Black Rock Desert: "Cattle have formed the character of the American cowboy. Old cowboys are usually sour, profane, disdainful and skeptical. Why? From dealing with obnoxious cows and homicidal horses. Everything that has been said about cowboys needs re-examining! Has anybody ever written that most cowboys have ulcers? Chuckwagon food, too much raw whiskey, bad water, but above all, worry and frustration from contending with the goddam cows."

No cowboy's character, of course, was solely the result of association with cows. His popular image is congeneric with the horse rather than with the critter, and it is from the former that he acquired much of the vulgarized glamour that has ossified into a mass fixation. Except for an occasional stampede or as something to be rustled, cows are nonessential in casting horse operas. Hitched outside saloons, horses stand braced for the flying mount (which Jean Daniels used to say "was a helluva lot less common around a cow outfit than the flying dismount"), the daring getaway in the cloud and clatter of dust and hoofs, the mad descent down the canyon wall, the splash across the ford, the scramble up the ridge, the prolonged pursuit over prairie, plain, pampas, and prickly pear. Nevertheless, it was the unruly critter that turned the horseman into a cowboy—a vaquero, a buckaroo.

This is not to say that the cowboy was bred to

this "cow culture" like a coyote to brush country. Charlie Russell's yarn about the Eastern girl who asked her mother, "Do cowboys eat grass?" pushes Darwin too far. Few original cowboys were born to the range. In the mid-nineteenth century, America was still predominantly agrarian, and forerunners of the breed were familiar with cows and horses long before they wandered westward. Veterans of the Confederate cavalry who seeped into Texas in time to exploit the ripening cattle trade were already sufficiently toughened to life in the saddle to acquire readily the skills of Mexican vaqueros. They learned even more from their bouts with the critters that haunted the thornbush and brandished horns that could span nine feet. Recruits to the burgeoning craft were boys who had been reared on Midwestern farms, in New England towns, or even in cities and villages of the Old World. Their basic character traits were already formed, and the cow country only appealed to the same impulses that led venturesome adolescents to run away to see or to join the circus. Once a "shorthorn" made his decision to throw in with a cow outfit, however, the vocation initiated an inexorable process of natural selection, weeding out those whose appetite for cowboying was quickly sated. Frank Harris lasted one drive and concluded the English edition of *On the Trail* by stating bluntly, "I had enough of cattle driving. . . ." Weeks of staring between a horse's twitching ears at the excrement caked on the backsides of calves faltering in the drags could snap a raw hand's mainspring. Jean Daniels used to claim that all it took to make a cowhand "was someone who could live without sleep, without grub, without water, and enjoyed taking his bath reg'lar in alkali dust." If tedium was broken, it was when a hand dabbed his rope on a thousand-pound critter for the first time and rapidly began figuring odds on whether he'd be jerked to the mending shack or the grave. A recruit who survived four seasons and was willing to sign on for another roundup had the makings of a cowboy. Even if he decided to "saddle the breeze," the intricacy and intensity of the relationship formed between man, animal, and the elements and the totally consuming nature of participation in the work of "the outfit" was an experience unlikely to fade from memory.

The spurious lessons Harris claimed to have picked up from his year working with cows were only moral embroidery for the American version of his *Reminiscences*. Such schoolbook virtues, if learned at all, could be acquired from any number of exacting occupations. The provocative question is "What peculiar breed did cowpunching produce—and why?" Not much sociological expertise is required to recognize that life in the briny deep, under the big top, or at home on the range would attract, repel, and temper individuals in different ways.

Aboard ship, marine discipline prevails. An able-bodied seaman whose response to authority resembled that of a cowboy would spend his life in the brig. Likewise, ambulatory carnivals catering constantly to the whims of the crowd demanded routines and attitudes which a cowboy would have found unbearable. Some similarity between the behavior of sailors on shore leave and cowboys loose on the town might be attested, but the comparison would be superficial. Drunken barroom brawls involving cowhands are products of banal literary imaginations. They despised fistic encounters and contemptuously labeled them "dogfights." The cowboy was almost fastidious about the care of his hands. He used them for roping, hog tying, earmarking and cutting, for braiding reatas, and for managing his horse. Many top hands wore gloves—except those like Jean Daniels who argued that growing new skin was cheaper. If a dispute had to go beyond an "augurin' match," the cowhand preferred a gun—not because he was eager to throw lead, but because it eliminated bodily contact and minimized physical inequalities. Unlike clumsy, prolonged pummeling with fists, a gun was dignified, its decisions quick and unequivocal. Besides, it wasn't often necessary to use it. Its visible presence alone had a sobering effect. Courtesy has gone out of fashion because discourtesy no longer incurs risk.

A cowboy's aversion to bodily contact was deeply rooted and closely related to a misanthropic element in his personality. He became accustomed to space and was exceptionally vulnerable to claustrophobia. Unlike ship's quarters, bunkhouses were roomy and usually contained accommodations for double the number of hands normally employed. When a cowhand threw down his bedroll, he was mighty particular about depositing it as far from an occupied bunk as possible. If he came too close to an incumbent, the latter was likely to order him gruffly to bed down some place else. (The cow country was proud of its tradition of hospitality, however, and sharing a bunk or bed was called "splitting the blanket." Henry Steen used to say, "I'll split my blanket with a hand any time so long as he uses his half when I ain't needin' it.") At the feed rack, the cowhand left an empty chair between himself and those already buried in their nose bags. Late arrivals were rarely forced to wedge themselves into a crevice. Tables in most cookhouses were lengthy, and even when full handed, there was usually a completely vacant end. Places were set, of course, for unexpected visitors, strays and drifters riding the chuck line, but this does not account for the diffusive disposal of space. The cowboy had an antipathy to crowding and congestion. Critters madding at water holes, shouldering and hooking each other at feed troughs, spilling and tromping more fodder into the mud than they greedily devoured, were objects of cynical disgust.

Contrary to common notions, the cowboy did not relish handling large herds. He preferred cattle spread out. The term "roundup" has become distorted in popular imagination. What made the roundup appealing to the cowboy was that it meant getting away from the home ranch and onto the open range. Most of the agreeable work consisted of riding alone over vast areas, flushing small bunches from isolated canyons, brakes, and meadows, and relocating them until the full herd had been gathered and the new calves cut out and branded—an immense Easter-egg hunt with critters for eggs.

Branding, too, has become vulgarly romanticized, largely as a consequence of exploiting it as a spectacle for the amusement of guests at dude ranches. To the cowboy, especially the ground crew, branding was an ordeal of inescapable dust, spurting blood, and the smell of burning flesh and hair. He preferred to hold, cut, and doctor the herd in the open. When corral branding and the squeeze chute replaced the open fire, the running iron, and the wagon on the unfenced range, the cowhand didn't relax until the gates were swung open and the impatient herd flooded onto the pasture and began to scatter out. Ed Fisher, the last range-bred cow boss of the Fiddleback, once branded the whole spring crop alone—a few head each day—out where the land hadn't been seeded to fence posts and where grass grew without an invitation. He had his horse, his rope, a piggin' string, a sawed-off iron, and he could get coals out of sagebrush. When we showed up around the first of June with a glorified sense of self-importance for the epic task ahead, the work of the roundup inconspicuously had been done. Ed was a cowboy.

Closely related to the cowboy's mild claustrophobia was his nonmalignant xenophobia. Whenever strangers appeared at the mess house of the Fiddleback, the normally garrulous hands would lapse into surly silence. If a visitor attempted to be sociable, the comments elicited after his departure were likely to be on the order of "that feller talked like his jaw was being attacked by heel flies." The cowboy was a loner by choice, and in a limited respect, he was a snob. He preferred the company of his horse and the peevish critter to that of humans (excepting the punchers he rode with—and then only if they didn't come too damn close).

The cowboy's most admirable possession was that uncommon virtue which, for some baffling reason, is called "common sense." As already indicated, around cow camps it is called "gumption," a refined crossbreeding of some questionable virtues with some unquestionable vices. Among the former were certainly stoicism, fortitude, skepticism, and a philosophical modesty that should not be confused with humility or diffidence. In the cowboy, this composite was definitely a product of prolonged working experience with stock. "There ain't nothin' a hand ever learned hisself about the critter that wouldn't be wrong," Jean Daniels would mutter wryly, expressing with a single brushstroke the essence of the attitude indicated above. Knowledge of the critter was a lore, not a science, because the animal's conduct, despite feral consistency, was fundamentally nonpredictable. In fact, the tendency of the animal's behavior to follow established patterns was what made its ultimate unpredictability exasperating and sometimes lethal. It could suddenly turn from Jekyll into Hyde—from a cow to a critter.

On one memorable occasion Holly and I were bringing a batch of recalcitrant heifers off the head of Reese River. The country is rough, precipitous, and the slopes of the steep canyons are strewn alternately with groves of mahogany and great patches of tightly matted quaking aspen. We wanted to bring them down into the relatively open stream bed of South

Twin. Cattle under herd in mountainous terrain have a tendency to set a brisk pace directly along the contours of the ridges. They are difficult to control, because they are picking the game trails while the rider is bounding about on his snorting horse, fighting brush and shale, trying to keep above and abreast of the leaders simultaneously. If a rider loses his bunch, they can skirt the side hills and slip over a divide into another drainage basin. If they ever emerge onto the flat, they can be forty miles from where he wanted them—over a hundred miles as a cowhorse travels and if they happen to be Fiddlebacks.

This bunch had made up its collective mind to elude us, but we had them outfoxed. We thought. Ahead was a mammoth talus slope about a quarter of a mile wide at the base and narrowing to a point at its apex. Between the peak of the talus and the foot of the cliff that rose sharply above it was a skirt of stunted aspen. If the leaders crashed this thicket before we headed them off, they could worm through the brush for Mexico. We could not have turned them, because there would have been no way to get in front of them. Hampered by the talus below and the cliff above, we could only helplessly have followed their tails. Cows make tunnels through thickets which afford them snug escape routes while horse and rider, their heads tangled in a network of branches, are effectively checked. The critters knew all this and were cunningly edging toward their little green gateway to freedom. But while they were reading our minds, we were reading theirs.

"Stay on their ass," Holly shouted confidently. "I'll scoot ahead. All we have to do is keep above 'em. When they hit that rockslide, they won't have no place to go but *down*."

I agreed. The talus slope was an effective barrier. It would have stopped a mountain goat.

Only it didn't stop our critters. The leaders hit the slide, hesitated while they eyed Holly poised vigilantly above, cast a backward glance at me, and proceeded to stumble deliberately into the rock.

"Them dirty, festerin', no-good, sonsabitching fodder-muckers. . . !" Holly cut loose a torrent of profanity that would stupefy the current generation that seems to suffer from the delusion that it discovered the four-letter word.

The critters reached the middle of the slide and came to a standstill. All we had to do was figure how to get them out. One thing for sure was that we didn't want them to continue across onto the far shore. They had to be brought *back*. We had two advantages. Goaded by a man on foot behind them, they could scent their way over their own tracks. Also, they would be enticed by the horses stationed at the edge of the slide as decoys. Even had the horses been able to mince their way through the slide without crippling themselves, they would have been no use to us in the rocks.

Holly argued that one of us should stick with his horse to prevent the critters from bolting uphill and into the quakers if they decided to come out, so I worked around the stranded cattle on foot to get into position to haze them back. They wouldn't budge.

They let me push, poke, prod, and lather their rumps with my coiled rope. No go. After meditation and consultation (we hadn't yet gotten around to prayer), we agreed that Holly's presence on his horse was spooking them. So he climbed down and joined me, leaving Roany with dropped reins in a spot that he could get to fast should the critters suddenly plunge out. Everything had been calculated as fine as a tanned snakeskin. Except that a half hour later when they began an unheralded exodus, they headed straight for *us*, ignoring our flailing ropes, our fanning hats, and our angry hollers. Right on past us they went, and out the far side as if we had been of no more account than a pair of juniper stumps. Off for the Matto Grosso. The Panama Canal wasn't going to stop them. Holly squatted down and *bawled*. My delirious laughter was akin to his tears.

We limped back to the horses, who nickered with sympathy. When it concerns the critter, a cow horse shares its rider's sentiments.

Hours later, as we neared camp, we met Jean descending another canyon with our runaways in tow. He'd spotted a plume of dust along the shoulder of a ridge where "it hadn't orter had been." He knew they were critters that had dodged some bedeviled rider and he cut their caper short. The way a top hand can appear from nowhere in time to stop the hanging is uncanny.

This episode was routine compared to many—some accompanied by sinister consequences. It should be clear, at any rate, that cowboy fortitude didn't come from the Boy Scout's manual. It was a product of constant confrontation with unreasoning reality. It was the only attitude left that made sense after every possible response to adversity—rage, disgust, self-pity—failed to pay off. Instead of hunting up a dog to kick, the cowboy learned to keep his wits in easy reach. He realized, too, that there were a lot of times when that "didn't help none neither." His thoroughgoing skepticism went so far as to support his innocent superstitions. "It may not do no good," Henry Steen admitted when Jean raked him over for tucking a rabbit's foot into his shirt pocket every time he climbed aboard a raw bronc, "but it sure don't do no harm."

Such clarity of perception was another ingredient of gumption, and the cowboy stuck to it. A situation which might appear to tender minds as one of desperation never drove a seasoned hand to the cracking point. He accepted fate without becoming a fatalist. Holly Richardson's mare dropped dead under him out by the potholes on the edge of the baking alkali flats. She'd become overheated, and he'd let her drink bad water. He stripped saddle, blanket, and bridle from the corpse and packed his gear fifteen miles across the naked grid. It was a scorching September day. "Creepin' jeezus," the cow boss exclaimed when Holly staggered into camp, "you should of left that slick-fork out there and gone back for it with a fresh horse and a mule."

"It give me sump'n to sit on when I got tired," Holly replied.

The horse had been from my string and usually a cowhand, though taciturn in the face of adversity, would have been inwardly riled by the abuse of one of his mounts, but the worst he would be likely to do would be to deliver the culprit some heavy, profane sarcasm reflecting on his competence as a hand, or give him the silent treatment until his "mad" wore off. Occasionally, as illustrated by an abnormally extended aphonic spell between Henry and Zane, the crew, following someone's inspired lead, would eventually intervene with wit and humor that neither of the stubbornly offending parties could withstand. Such instances were few. The mental and physical demands made upon everyone by daily confrontation with critters quickly dissolved personal feuds.

The death or suffering of any animal (except critters) immediately sets my heart to hemorrhaging, but Black Susie had been foisted on me as the mail-order cowboy, and although I had an affection for the clumsy brute, she'd bankrupted my self-esteem on countless occasions. "Well, Doc, guess you got yourself a new carvin' horse," Jean remarked in the middle of our evening chuck—at which everyone allowed himself to be swept aloft by his own mirth. Susie, as they all knew, couldn't cut a lame cow from a corral with the fences down. She had been given to me one day when I had insisted on trying my hand at trimming the herd instead of contenting myself with my customary job of holding the cut. I never got rid of her—a fitting punishment for premature enthusiasm.

"At least the coyotes should throw a good litter of spring pups," Henry said. "Susie packed enough lard to feed 'em all winter." After which banter we all loped to Carver's where I loaded Holly with drinks as a token of the fact that I bore him no grudge. Holly was not booze-broke and he rode away from there freighting a head made to fit a pack-mule. Some of the crew suspected me of having taken a bushwhacker's revenge. "I didn't know he was there when I started shooting," I emphatically maintained.

Around a cow outfit, grumbling was managed without surrendering composure. Closely related to Jean's law of indeterminacy, as derived from the nature of the critter, was the more general observation "Nothin' never gets so bad it can't get plumb worse." The time Henry got himself ripped up by a mad cow before she could be choked down and dragged from the corral, Carl Haas delivered up the conventional cliche. "Could of been worse," he said as Henry's segments were gathered into the pickup and hauled off to the Tonopah Hospital.

"Yeah," Holly solemnly agreed, "he could of been kilt."

"Worser than that," Carl added, "it could of been me."

The cowboy never indulged in useless and insincere pity, but faced with a grim situation he could be counted upon to contribute more than tea and sympathy. Nevertheless, virtues are counterparts of certain inverse traits inappropriately called vices. To avoid leaving posterity with an unbalanced portrait of the cowboy's character, some of these negative qualities warrant attention. In short, we must look at the cowboy as a "critter."

iii

Stoicism can manifest itself as intractability—if not downright stubbornness. Healthy skepticism, properly weathered, is indistinguishable from cynical irreverence. The measured modesty that is a by-product of the uncertainty principle is a source of much of the cowboy's misanthropic exclusiveness and of his distrust of everything institutional. Iron fortitude, appearing without fanfare and often garbed like a rodeo clown, can improperly be interpreted as soulless inclemency. Gumption was as much a compound of these unseemly imperfections as it was of impeccable virtue. Probably more. Overdoses of faith, hope, and charity could dehorn a hand in a hurry.

Mother Nature is not one of religion's effective missionaries. Atheists may or may not have occupied foxholes, but it can be stated with certainty that a high tally of infidels could be run up among those who rode the range. Routine cattle work presented riders with so many grisly tasks and so much horror that the notion of justice, sacred or profane, was plainly absurd. A compassionate deity was as comprehensible as a softhearted horsefly. The same brand of rational empiricism that supported Henry Steen's defense of his rabbit's foot led the cowboy to reject the existence of God but to acknowledge the existence of the Devil. "Evidence is a mite lean fer the former, but a hand wouldn't have no trouble proving up his claim fer the latter," Jean Daniels would argue during sessions of cow-camp theology.

The range presented an inexhaustible record of unwitnessed tragedy. Everywhere, withered hides clung to the crumbling scaffoldings of gray-white bones—midget tents pitched across the arid wasteland, visited only by the ubiquitous magpie and other scavengers of the purple sage. Carcasses in bogs, ravines, and caved-in mine shafts, carcasses heaped against corners of drift fences where blizzard-trapped animals, their backs to the scourging wind, perished in mass misery, carcasses strewn around water holes baked into yellow crusts by years of drought, carcasses in the buckbrush, in swampy meadows, amid the mountain timber—these and countless other testaments to the savagery of the elements constantly sharpened the cowboy's awareness of the harshness of life. The surface inclemency of the cowhand was a psychological neccessity. His morbid wit cloaked repressed sensitivity. It was a defiant assertion of immunity to the outrages perpetrated by the forces of evil and a device for scoring a moral victory over them.

Management at the Fiddleback assaulted the ecological equilibrium in Smoky Valley by combining the flow of North and South Twin Rivers into a six-mile concrete ditch to carry the streams in a direct line across the alluvial fan to the newly extended alfalfa fields below. The purpose was to reduce water loss from percolation and evaporation. Riding near the outlet of this new sluice channel one day during the spring runoff, I spotted a group of calves kneeling as if in prayer. Calves are no more prone to piety than cowhands—it was a flagrantly unnatural posture. Moreover, there were no cows in sight, so I loped over to see what was up. As I approached, they made no attempt to scatter—which was unusual. Suddenly the situation became sickeningly clear. Staring at me from the pond were six calves with their front legs sheared off at the knee joints. While drinking from the upper end of the ditch, they had been swept off their feet by the swift current. Cows get up by folding their front legs under them and hoisting their hindquarters erect—the reverse of a horse. The small calves hadn't been able to follow through against the force of the water, and their slender legs had been worn off by friction against the abrasive concrete. There was nothing to do but ride to the ranch, pick up a rifle, and put them out of misery.

Watching cattle sink helplessly into quicksand, or plunge to destruction over rimrock, or "die-up" during blizzards, or drown while swimming rivers was a significant feature of the cowboy's job which seldom receives treatment in western fiction except as a melodramatic episode adding thrilling touches to a thoroughly implausible plot. These experiences were far from colorful to the cowboy, and his commentary upon them was restricted to the immediate circle of his fellow riders. If he did not brood over them, he reflected upon them privately, and they shaped his philosophical attitudes. Remorse was regarded as futile self-indulgence. Yet it would be a mistake to assume that the cowboy lacked a sense of justice. He possessed one—subtle and profound.

In unusual (poetic) circumstances when justice appeared to take a hand in the game, the cowboy greeted it with enthusiasm, but continued to regard the intercession as accidental. Justice simply lacked a will of its own. One had the choice of leaving the day of reckoning to chance, or acting as the self-appointed agent of destiny. Justice was something that had to be *applied*. By *someone*. Because of his misanthropic and empirically justifiable distrust of most humans and of *all* institutions, the cowboy figured he'd have to secure justice himself. "Justice," remarked a former saddlemate after having shot a porcupine whose quills, I protested, could not have been identified as the ones protruding from an unfortunate calf's nose, "is what I personally dish out." This attitude should not be construed to mean that the cowboy advocated taking the law into his own hands. "Law" was another critter. Its coincidence with justice was also accidental, and the cowboy placed no confidence in it. The attitude explains such synonyms for the six gun as a *one-eyed judge, peacemaker, equalizer, talking iron, peerless persuader,* and the like. It eliminated hairsplitting. It could blaze a quick trail to heaven and give a hand the down payment on a halo. But the cowboy was never an easy recruit for a lynch mob. Quite the contrary. His misanthropy rendered him suspicious of lynching parties as well as of courts, and his intrinsic skepticism made him wary of premature judgments. He was no bigot. When he eventually acquired a conviction, it was usually a sound one.

When meting out justice, the cowboy shared jurisdiction with his horse. That is, the horse cooperated as an active partner rather than as a mindless vehicle used to pursue escaping rustlers. The ease with which a cow horse seemed to subscribe to the same code as its rider even confounded old gristle-heels long accustomed to equine intelligence. Horses would bite the rumps of sluggards loitering in the drags. They were selective in applying the persuasive power of their teeth and hoofs. I have seen them bite ill-mannered steers and gently nudge small calves. Anecdotes recounting the judicial and punitive expertise of celebrated cow horses offered fertile opportunities for what was called "blanket stretching." To the cowboy, his horse was a peer. Consequently, it was never referred to as a critter unless a hand wished to insult it in the same manner with which he sometimes referred to the cook (when the latter was well out of earshot).

A considerable quantity of literature, some of it presumably serious, has portrayed the cowboy as an individual with scant regard for life—a sort of upland gangster type. Actually, he prized life highly, but his acute awareness of its brevity, brutality, and uncertainty prevented him from treating it as though it were pheasant under glass. He didn't consecrate life; he lived it while he had the chance. His work required the five senses to be constantly on point. Alertness became a habit, and he lived his full life accordingly. There were no middle-aged cowboys. Middle-age is a condition of urbanite despair to which cowboy life was immune. If a hand survived the follies of infancy and adolescence and lived to be thirty, he'd learned enough to carry himself into his eighties without surrendering much vigor, stamina, or gumption. He was capable of packing his ulcers around with him for years. *Cuidado* ("Beware!") was not a word a cowboy admitted into his vocabulary with casual indifference. He learned it from the vaquero, and the critter reminded him of it every day. It should not be forgotten that the cowboy was a craftsman, and the true craftsman is *never careless*. It was because the cowboy understood and respected chance that he refused to trust it. Chance was a critter. When cowboys gambled, they were prepared to lose.

Zest, alertness and vitality are not qualities to be measured on a scale. They are absolutes. When they are gone, the kid from Laredo lies cold as the clay. A story is told of a Tonopah preacher who was delivering a funeral sermon over the casket of an old range veteran long and widely known in Nye County. The garrulous clergyman was waxing unctuously elequent. "Old Dan is not dead," he declared, "he has just taken the highest trail. . . ." The sardonic voice of another old puncher sounded from a rear pew of the church, "I got a hundred sez he's dead!"

Gumption, stripped of excess tallow, is the ability to stare down the double-barrel of reality and offer it the best possible deal.

iv

There are still ranch hands and there are still cows, but there are clearly no longer cowboys and no longer critters. The two were mutually dependent upon each other, and they hit the highest trail together. The critter, as usual, took the lead. The Longhorn was replaced by domestic breeds. Deprived of freedom to roam, bred and crossbred to shorten legs and increase body weight to the point that were it again forced to fend for itself on open range it would fail to survive, the cow deteriorated into a mobile vegetable. Shorn of its horns by carpentry, chemistry, and genetics—turned into what cowhands used to contemptuously call a "muley"—branded and doctored in squeeze chutes, glutted with hay, grain, and feed supplement, and marketed before it reached its prime, this pitiful, hothouse nullity has no chance to become a mature cow, let alone a critter. The extinction of the critter, more than any other factor, doomed the cowboy. The symbiotic relationship that made them into a spectacular combination was categorically destroyed. The challenges that produced the cowboy vanished and the skills he had perfected survived only as "stunts" to be performed under conditions in no way reproducing those of the range.

The historian's duty is to rescue the past from abuse by the present—a difficult task. Academic scholarship is worth about as much as a four-card flush when it comes to instilling its subject with living tissue. But despite their lifeless abstractions, documented fables, and denatured fantasies, professional historians have been less malign in their treatment of the cowboy than have producers of film and fiction. The latter have made the cowboy preposterous. He was not a dancing bear, a gun-slinging buffoon, or a handsome heroic ham. The top hands I have known would have felt less ill at ease in a mausoleum than in the Cowboy Hall of Fame. The cowboy did not need synthetic glamour to give him stature. His stature emerged from the proud practice of his craft, not from drinking prowess, the fast draw, or the ten-gallon hat. The cowboy did not wear a *costume*. He dressed for work. Jean Daniels never owned a Stetson. He cherished the striped caps that engineers on steam locomotives used to wear. He spent most of his ground time welding busted ranch equipment and pacifying his ulcer with sour mash. He roped underhand from Whitey, an all-around cow horse with a back like the initial of this writer's last name. "Him and Whitey together," Henry Steen used to say, "is too thin to throw a shadow!" Jean always hind-footed his critter, and I seldom saw him spill a loop. He was a cowboy.

"The Old Sonovabitch don't need me to practice on no more," Jean once remarked with a somber, chuckling cough. We were chewing raw turnips and discussing a favorite range topic, the ceaseless activity and energy of the Devil. "There's plenty more critters left in the corral fer him to rope." It was the only time I'd ever heard the old man utter anything that savored of self-pity, and at the time I was puzzled and a speck uncomfortable. A few days later he put a shotgun in his mouth and blew his head off. It was an act of neither cowardice nor despair. There was an element of humorous scorn revealed by the gesture that it is impossible for me to depict. He wasn't defiant, but he didn't intend to await slow starvation with the onset of winter snows, and he wasn't going to remain stove up in a Reno hospital dependent upon the petulant attention of others. He knew that sick people are secretly hated. Jean had plenty of gumption. In his way, he was a hero.

the Maverick

Before turning the maverick loose from the chute, I must quote a passage containing the most commendable advice ever offered to a prospective writer other than that he should throw his saddle in the wagon and head for town. The passage consists of the two opening paragraphs of Cyril Connolly's *The Unquiet Grave* which he published under the sobriquet, Palinurus.

> The more books we read, the sooner we perceive that the true function of a writer is to produce a masterpiece and that no other task is of any consequence. Obvious though this

> should be, how few writers will admit it, or having made the admission, will be prepared to lay aside the piece of iridescent mediocrity on which they have embarked! Writers always hope that their next book is going to be their best, for they will not acknowledge that it is their present way of life which prevents them from ever creating anything different or better.
>
> All excursions into journalism, broadcasting, propaganda and writing for the films, however grandiose, are doomed to disappointment. To put our best into these forms is another folly, since thereby we condemn good ideas as well as bad to oblivion. It is in the nature of such work not to last, so it should never be undertaken. Writers engrossed in any literary activity which is not their attempt at a masterpiece are their own dupes and, unless these self-flatterers are content to write off such activities as their contribution to the war effort, they might as well be peeling potatoes.

Citing these noble words does not imply that the following exegesis on the maverick was undertaken with the intent to produce a masterpiece or, at the opposite end of the scales, neither was it written as an exercise in composing a piece of iridescent mediocrity. Along with Wilde, Cabell and a number of other mandarins, I incline to the opinion that iridescence if not incompatible with some symptoms of mediocrity may at least vindicate it. This raises a literary problem in the intrinsic relationship between style and content. Can a writer perfect one without the other? Or, more pertinent to the subject of this book, can a star rodeo performer excell in every event and fail as a cowboy? The essay was not exactly an excursion into journalism, but it could be regarded as a contribution to the war effort. While readers mentally ask, "What war?" they can also cogitate on their own answers to the preceding questions.

Admittedly, however, "The Maverick" was conceived in sin. It was written originally upon request for the May, 1969 issue of *The American West.* Roger Olmsted, having advanced to the rank of Editor, again played his role of Mephisto. The Ford Motor Company was about "to stampede the little-car market" with one of its periodic crossbreeds, the *Maverick*, and had appropriately purchased advertising space in the befitting periodical. A photograph entitled *Goodbye Old Paint* featured a leathery buckaroo and his pinto posing by the sleek "motorized steed." Beneath was a sub-caption, "Among the several non-conformist colors being offered to purchasers of the Maverick are Anti-EstablishMint, Freudian Gilt, and Thanks Vermillion." Roger thought it a cosmic idea if the issue carrying this momentous ad were to run a lead-article simultaneously on the celebrated critter whose name the dashing new model was to bear. Would I write such an article - fast? Roger, a true-and-tried Westerner, had visions of the Big Bonanza, the Lost Dutchman Mine, the Seven Cities of Cibola. . . the advertising division of Ford Motor

Company would rocket into orbit. They would order a minimum of a hundred thousand reprints to distribute to their salesmen and customers. We would be rich.

Roger's scheme was flawed. He had forgotten the talent of the author of "Cowboys, Cow Horses and Cows" for alienating the mass-man. He recognized that advertising departments will spend money lavishly for almost any fatuous gimmick, but failed to grasp the simple fact that they would balk at grubstaking their avowed assassins. He was overconfident in the law of institutional inertia according to which corporations endorse suicidal policies because there are so many conflicting jurisdictions in operation that infelicitous programs acquire the stamp of official approval before some chance company maverick has the luck to spot it and the sanity to trap it. Although I was not in quest of gold, glory or the grail, I seized the opportunity to try to take the slack out of the rope of whatever Harvard-type MBA co-opted hallowed titles like "maverick" and "mustang" to glamorize the most ubiquitous, insidious and sinister enemies of civilized transportation devised by our amaurotic technologists. Palinurus could conceivably class this encomium on the maverick as propaganda.

Mavericks and mustangs are both entities that derived luster from their initial association with the "wide open spaces" and the frontier tradition. The ambivalent meanings these words have assumed through common usage is one of the myriad examples of history as amphigory. As metaphors, early use of the terms simply indicated a maverick as an alien and a mustang as someone without breeding. Whether a creditable or discreditable connotation was implied depended entirely upon the attitudes of the users. The social democracy of the frontier propounded by Frederick Jackson Turner conspicuously elevated the status of many appelations of derogatory origin. Urban society and the modern industrial state is once again reversing the process.

From "alien," *maverick* began to be used as a synonym for an "outsider," or a "loner," or any perverse individual who insisted upon going against the grain - concisely illustrated by my late father, a bank president and no maverick-lover, in his summation of his only-begotten son's character. "The trouble with Owen is he thinks the whole world is out of step but him." Such renditions are all negativistic in the sense that they convey withdrawal, secession and disgruntled self-exclusion from the social order. Nevertheless, the maverick is very much a part of this world - especially in his splendid isolation. This brings to the surface a sequence of engaging paradoxes. But Ed Fisher is sending up his smoke signals. I can hear his voice from out of the past announcing on some sub-zero morning when he figured we had played the pot long enough, "Well, fellers, it's time to break jail."

There were no mavericks on the Fiddleback. Why not? Because they were all mavericks. This is analogous to the old logic-befuddler, "if a tree falls in the forest and no one is there to hear it, is there a noise?" When I dabbed this hooley-ann on Jean he jerked me clean out of the saddle. "As far as I'm concerned," he replied tersely, "there ain't." After that I learned to take my turns around the horn quick instead of heedlessly holding the end of the rope in my hand. Damn it! I should have said "sound" instead of "noise" and I might have had him. . .

From the owner, Emma Rogers, to the bucketman, Ray Wiggins, every member of the outfit was as unique as an Indian brand. Wiggins fed the chickens and salvaged what eggs he could from the skunks and civet cats. He milked four dairies, did the separating, hoarded the cream, churned butter that never had the sour tang washed out of it and made cottage cheese as rough and dry as coarse sawdust. He emptied slop to the pigs, voluntarily tended a small vegetable garden and produced a tomato in 1954 almost ripe enough to harvest before the first freeze claimed it. He waged a heroic losing battle against sardonic predators. Wiggins also served as cook except for those halycyon interludes when Emma's mercy felleth as the gentle rain from heaven upon those of us beneath and she decided we deserved an edible meal.

Wiggins was neither regarded nor treated as a menial because every member of the crew lived in fear and trembling that he might light a shuck and who then would draw the low card that condemned him to be Wiggins' successor until some thumb-riddled, barely adequate replacement could be found? Not that Wiggins' duties were in themselves onerous, but they were tyrannous and whoever found himself afflicted with them felt reduced to ritualized servitude. Anyone rash enough to offer to spell the bucket-man for a single day risked condemning himself to permanent slavery - as Hercules learned to his chagrin when he relieved Atlas of the burden of holding up the sky. I *was* an expert at milking cows and enjoyed listening to that steady, forceful, satisfying stream surging into the pail achieved by the masterful, rhythmic coordination of finger-pressure instead of the feeble, amateurish, intermittent splashes of some inept novice performing as though he were trying to produce a urine specimen to put out a fire. But I kept my skill a secret.

Wiggins, fortunately for all of us, exulted in his role. He preferred the majestic Hegelian form of Freedom as the fulfillment of one's destiny to the snivelling Benthamite view of freedom as the absence of vindicable restraints. As the outfit's scapegoat, he stoically endured considerable chaffing. It only augmented his self-esteem and he thought of himself not as a goat, but as a glorified Judas-steer. Emma, who badgered him more ferociously than anyone, possessed his unquestioning loyalty. Was she not the fountain-head of his moral authority? He was the one detailed to rouse the crew long before the crack of dawn which he always did with unnecessary zeal, regularity, clatter and the sadistic clarion call, "Rise and shine!" He was the one with despotic authority over the menu and his disagreeable lack of culinary imagination was exceeded in distastefulness only by those instances when he exercised it. "Wiggins' Goulash" was the mildest phrase applied to his odious concoctions. He was the one instructed to keep locks on the pantry, the meat-house, the spud-cellar and the gas pump. One day I happened to be conversing with Emma when Zane approached the veranda.

"Excuse me, Miss Emma," he said, obviously repressing a seething rage beneath surface politeness, "my heap is plumb empty and I wanted to borrow enough juice to get me to Tonopah, but that goddamn Wiggins has the pump locked again. When I asked him to open it he had the guts to tell me I drew enough wages to buy my own gas in town."

"Hmmph!" Emma serenely continued to fan herself and rattle the loose boards of the porch with her steady rocking. "You tell that skinflint that I said for him to give you the key and for you to go help yourself. And next time you ask me for something, don't use that deceitful word "borrow." That way you'll be able to stay honest."

"Yes, ma'am." Zane spread his plumage and took off like a righteous Mormon on his way to an infidel's hanging. "Be sure to return the key to Ray when you're through with it," she called after him.

Unable to resist an impulse to make Emma grab the horn, I waited until Zane was well beyond earshot and then said, "Hell, Emma, you're the one who tells Ray to keep that gas-pump locked and then you go out of your way to make him look like the ranch villain. How come?"

"That's what I pay him for," Emma snapped. "You ask fool questions."

I've thought that one over several times. Everyone had nothing but good words for 'Miss Emma.' No one had anything good to say about Wiggins. And everyone, including Ray and Zane, was kept happy.

No one nursed grudges or allowed rats to gnaw at their innards. All was harmony. Pure chance set me to punching cows on the Fiddleback. And I found myself part of a community in which I was in step with everyone and everyone seemed to be in step with me. "What sort of a world would it be if everyone thought and acted the way you do?" was one of my well-intentioned father's favorite questions when we'd both get on the prod. "Someone has to accept responsibilities."

Well, I concluded at the time on the basis of my theoretical premises, it would be a damned site better world than the one I was inhabiting. Fifty years later I find myself of the same opinion - experience having come to fill the breach between theory and practice. I became a member of a society of mavericks - and it was the only time in my life I was free to conduct myself according to my own standards without reprisals. I had companions instead of associates. But I don't want to spill my loop by making the toss too soon. So far we only have the subject of the maverick by its tail and haven't figured out how to handle him or what to do with him. But we can't let go of that tail!

ii

Too many pack-outfits have ridden this country and littered the trails. It is necessary to blaze some fresh ones.

The *maverick* is not a recluse or a reject from organized community life as a consequence of his personal psychoneurosis. He is an independent spirit who avoids becoming bogged to the saddle-skirts in conventional mire, a proud renegade who assumes Promethean stature and lives by a dynamic code of honor in disregard and contempt of atrophied institutional morality. The *maverick* is the rebel against the gods of the multitude, Milton's defiant Satan - glorious especially in defeat - a creative, integrated, compulsively self-reliant personality type with which the West, factual and fictional, was as speckled as a spotted hound. Jack Slade, Jesse James, Billy the Kid, Ross McEwen, Shane and even that ultra-modern Hud are but a few specimens of this recalcitrant breed. Whether he operates inside or outside the law is, at this stage of the analysis, of secondary importance. The *maverick* is a natural aristocrat. He is not out of step with society. Society *is* out of step with him because society in the mass is in the drags of the mainstream of civilization. Despite the frequent irreverent and apparently reprehensible aspects of his external conduct, the *maverick* is the seed-bearer and essential core of all ethical cultures. Inside him burns celestial fire. He rides "the point."

This panegyric consciously assumes the dimensions of myth, but it is myth still picketed to reality somewhere near the summit of the pass. For a limited time, Samuel Augustus Maverick, 1803-1870, acquired a legendary reputation. The scarcity of authentic supermen in daily life compels us to create them, either by indulging pure fantasy or, as was the case in the transmogrification of Sam Maverick, by embellishing some meager fragment of fact. But while the world produces a willing supply of poetic liars, stimulated by visions of secular and spiritual gallantry who are eager to undertake the task, it also produces an equal number of industrious debunkers avid in their acrimonious desire to clip the eagle's wings and to depict the "truth" in its consoling, earthbound, dowdy sobriety.

Whether Art is superior to Life or Life superior to Art; whether Art ceases when hokum takes over; and whether hokum ever serves a useful purpose, are often baffling questions. As an historian, I am dedicated to the ascertainable facts, but as a living human being I appreciate the inspirational power of myth. I am familiar with the sophisticated cliches employed by scholastic minds for elucidating philosophical problems without resolving them. I am aware, for example, that myths can be relegated to certain categories of fact; that historians never deal with facts, but only with "evidence" of facts and that consequently history is a manipulation of evidence and therefore the fabrication of myth; that myth is an *extension* of fact; that Art, which incorporates myth, is actually an aspect of life and either distorts reality (another slippery word) to the detriment of "literal truth," or enhances it in the interest of a higher "creative truth"; and finally that these issues should be outlawed as "non-operationally" significant - in other words, meaningless - because conclusions drawn from discussion of them are not referable to any system of "scientific" verification.

These remarks are only designed to scare off intellectual coyotes whose logical stipulations, circumlocutions, linguistic refinements and general fringe-snapping would prevent us from getting any issues corraled. This discourse is not concerned with putting an iron on Truth, Reality, Art, Life and all their corollary ambiguities. It is concerned only with shedding light on a zone of moral friction and paradox underlying a deceptively innocent metamorphosis in the meaning of a word. The western frontier has been a popular battleground for impetuous champions of fiction and tenacious defenders of fact. The mutations in the term *maverick* and its ultimate extravagant transfiguration into the concept of "The Maverick" is only a single instance in which skirmishes between romantics and realists mask a basic conflict between ethical and material values within a society.

Once again, I scent a smoke signal by recalling Ed Fisher's comment when we picked up Henry after the fifth or sixth time he was grassed trying to uncork the same bronc. "There's some fellers that it don't matter how many times you spring them from the slammer, they'll always figure out a way to get back in."

Jean nodded upward. "He was dead set on forkin' that there cloud. One of these days he might make it."

iii

Sam Maverick's legend took root, and its pollen spread like ragweed. Around the campfires of the open range he became a cattle-titan whose glories were elaborated by loose-lipped cowhands with neither access to, nor interest in, the humble facts.

From an enterprising stockman, he was exhalted into an intrepid rogue, favored by Fate, possessed of demonic genius, and shrewdly inspired to record a slick-ear and a brandless brand, thereby laying claim to all critters roaming the great western ranges that had managed to elude roundup crews of the West's multifarious outfits, great or small. Compared to the crimpy shenanigans of the tin-bellied rascals who hung around the courthouses recording in their own names brands that uninitiated newcomers, through ignorance, had neglected to record for themselves, Maverick was an audacious giant. Rivaling Tchichikov, Gogol's picaresque scoundrel who made a fortune roping "Dead Souls," Maverick needed only to send his "reps" to the roundups of the major spreads, allow them to slouch in their saddles until all branded stock had been cut out, and instruct them to drive off with the remainder. A herd of such magnitude required commensurate property, which was easily conjured into existence by those who kept a loose cinch on their spirited jaws. Sam Maverick became the most stupendous landholder on the continent. He could cross the Republic of Texas without setting foot off his own land.

Such preposterousity could not pass unchallenged forever. In 1885, Charlie Siringo's *Autobiography* contemptuously brushed off Sam Maverick as a "chicken-hearted old rooster who wouldn't brand or earmark any of his cattle." But extravagant yarns persisted, and in 1889 George M. Maverick, the morally indignant son of the now notoriously renowned cattle baron, found it necessary for the repose of his own pious soul to refute "an erroneous, not to say atrocious, account" of his father's activities that had appeared in the St. Louis *Republic.* Not only was Sam Maverick innocent of the bucolic extravaganzas attributed to him, he was not even a cattleman! He was a graduate of Yale—thoroughly respectable insofar as a Texas attorney, businessman, and land speculator could be considered such—and a patriotic citizen whose public-spirited signature graced the Texas Declaration of Independence. In 1845 Sam Maverick had inadvertently acquired four hundred head of nondescript cattle in payment of an apparently otherwise uncollectable $1,200 debt. Knowing no way to dispose profitably of animals worth less than their hides, he turned them over for management to his "free" slave, later to achieve anonymous recognition in Durham and Jone's *Negro Cowboy* as one of the first black cowhands—though a slothful and inefficient one.

Maverick's black servant was no more a cowhand than his master was a cowman, and the cattle were abandoned to graze for themselves, unmolested by knife or iron. So astute a cattleman was Sam Maverick that eleven years later, in 1856, he wrote a bill of sale for an identical four hundred head to the brother of General Beauregard for $2,400, believing himself to have made a handsome profit. Assuming that after eleven years most of the original branded cows would have drifted into the pastures of heaven, before having done so they would have left ample progeny to multiply. With even a modest rate of increase (many of his "steers" having matured into mustang bulls), Sam Maverick should have possessed a herd of over fifty thousand head. If any party to the transaction can be considered demonically inspired, it was not honest Sam Maverick but A. Toutant Beauregard, who purchased the prolific unbranded herd and, presumably, squeezed the limit from his bargain. Thus the most stupefying part of the maverick legend disappears down a badger hole.

iv

Instead of being the Napoleon of the range-cattle industry, Sam Maverick was a pedestrian Texas bourgeois who, in the words of the Lone Star historian, John Henry Brown, was "a true and good man" who never grasped the stock of other people, but "allowed other people to appropriate his own young cattle till his herd ceased to be." But the glamour of the term did not perish with the glamour of the man. The unbranded critter rather than the well-branded owner slowly emerged as the symbol of rugged independence—that virtue so extolled by hard-core westerners. Within a decade after Maverick's sale of his unbranded stock, the term *maverick* had spread throughout the West as the name for unmarked animals that, ostensibly, were without owners and could lawfully be seized by anyone. The rapidity with which the term was exploited was due to the great number of wild cattle running loose in the brush and on the plains in the sixties and seventies. Others besides Maverick frequently neglected to brand calves; and cattle, like horses, flourished in an environment that supported vast herds of unbranded bison. When the railroads came and a sufficiently accessible and lucrative market appeared to encourage their profitable extermination, the maverick disappeared simultaneously with the bison. By 1884 associations of stockmen were attempting to outlaw "mavericking" which had become indistinguishable from rustling. Authentic wild cattle were extinct. Even without a brand most calves could be identified. They followed branded mothers, grazed on a home range, or shared the range with the stock of legitimate operators who could always divide the unbranded animals fairly during the common roundups. Little difficulty would be encountered in locating a critter's legal owner if one were inclined to do so. "Mavericks-ers," in order to remain in business, were compelled to create mavericks artificially by increasingly complicated methods such as slitting the tongues of calves so they could not suck, or rasping their feet so they could not follow, or slaughtering the mothers and trying to hide the hides. "Mavericking," as happens to varied forms of crime under capitalism, became such hard work that it either vanished or became incorporated into the marginal operations of legitimate producers. Its decline was not due to a rise in the standard of frontier morality. In fact, far from rising, frontier morality was in a state of eclipse. A new code was coming to the West.

In 1942, when Reese River, which can normally "be drunk dry by a single thirsty cow," reached flood stage, George Russell, owner of the 25 Ranch out of Battle Mountain, was compelled to turn twelve hundred unbranded calves loose on the public range or equip them with life-jackets. All twelve hundred were seized by neighbors in a rampage of greed unsurpassed since the opening of the Cherokee Strip. The incident typifies the change in the moral climate of the cattle community not because of the wholesale theft of the calves, but because Russell's "neighbors"—a word that at one time had implied traits other than mere residential proximity—took unscrupulous advantage of his adversity. Instead of volunteering friendly assistance to the victim of the sort of natural catastrophe that could have befallen any of them they behaved worse than magpies lighting on a wounded animal. Had gun-play not gone out of fashion, several fresh plantings could have taken place in the valley that spring and Jean Daniels would have been kept busy hammering at his box-shuck coffins. "Defenseless" is defined by Ambrose Bierce as "unable to attack." Being in that condition Russell would probably have survived, but the looters could have taken reasonable toll on each other as they snarled over the spoils and middling justice might have been done. Can anybody admissibly ask for more?

According to the *Fiddleback Almanac* long-ears weren't considered "mavericks" before they were lost, and helping a calf to get lost was considered the act of a cowhand whose tail was dragging. There were circumstances, however, in which appropriation of the untended stock of another outfit could be done with a stainless conscience and without need to claim the appropriated property by speciously labeling them "mavericks." Failure of an owner to take adequate care of his cows through inexcusable negligence can be advanced as a case in point. A "long-yearling" unbranded and unweaned is strong evidence of the carelessness, laziness and incompetence of some two-legged varmint. To take the adolescent parasite into custody is to do the mother cow a humane service. One overblown shirt-tail outfit that had drift rights on the Fiddleback range seemed habitually to run several cows that had two calves sucking at the same time. Coming across one of those churlish louts robbing the half-starved little fellow and draining the mother of milk and energy until she resembled the skeleton of an abandoned wickiup would put an arch in a hand's back and start his bristles pointing skyward. There would be only one thing to do and that was to wean the sonovabitch on the spot. And that meant hazing him so far away from his mother he'd never find his way back. And the only safe way to do that was to hustle him into a stout Fiddleback corral. Some stockmen deserved friendly assistance in their efforts to go belly-up.

Episodes illustrating line-camp justice as dispensed by Fiddleback knights-errant are swampy subjects for abstract generalization and carry conviction only in the context of their occurence. While readers wait expectantly for that to happen in *The Leather Throne,* I am on firm ground stating that no member of the crew held flabby doubts concerning the differences between right and wrong. It would be a mistake to conclude from this, however, that they were narrow minded and opinionated. There were no bigots on the Fiddleback. Life loped along smoothly even when the country got rough - especially when the country got rough. Riding rough country was their business.

The primary reason why an atmosphere of moral clarity prevailed was not on account of sunshine, clean air, pure streams, majestic mountains and great open spaces that expanded the soul - many petty bastards thrive in nature's scenic wonderlands - but because personal ethics and sensible customs took priority over dubious sanctions such as sin, mindless moral creeds and statute law. The last category was generally considered so confusing, conflicting, contradictory and contrary that it was worthless to anyone but a scoundrel. Jean described the legal system as "a pit regularly filled with enough snakes to keep a whole pack of law-wranglers fat chewing on them without ever having to turn out a decent day's work." One didn't "break the law." One ignored it. Ed Fisher's opinion, less acridly expressed, concurred with Jean's. "Any time you hang your hat on the peg of the law, don't expect it to be there when you get back."

This explains why cowhands wore their hats while eating in public cafes. It wasn't because they were ignorant or ill-mannered. They just didn't know a safer place for it than on their heads.

Fiddleback skepticism was eminently sane and was observed even by passionate temperaments. Tolerance was not a skim-milk attitude that makes timid creatures want to disappear down a dog-hole when they smell hide burning in a cooley at the wrong time of the day and in the wrong season. The old cowboy rule, "Never meddle in nothin' that don't bother you," doesn't argue that "nothin' should never bother you." What was important was to know which things one should be intolerant of - an ingredient that has disappeared from contemporary educational philosophy. It is probably just as well since educators could not be trusted to make the right judgments anyhow. Jean once phrased the same thought while expounding on a related topic. "There's a lot of sonsabitches that oughta be strung up, but I'm agin' capital punishment because they'd hang the wrong fellers." *Toleration* was not *professed* on the Fiddleback, but *tolerance* was *practiced.* No man's authority was accepted as gospel in areas of mutual human ignorance. Cowhands knew those areas.

Fiddleback punchers were self-broke. They were the real mavericks that we will eventually slap a brand on that won't wash off. Sometimes their independent spirit appears more on'ry than an overloaded pack-mule, but only because outsiders fail to appreciate the flawless logic of the uncorrupted minds of both mules and cowhands. Henry,in a state of exasperation during a thorny argument with Jean, finally accused the old man of being so stubborn that he wouldn't shift camp for a grass-fire.

"I'd wait to see if the wind was going to change," Jean answered abruptly.

V

By the middle of the present century true mavericks,

like every feature of range culture, belonged to the misunderstood past. Modern ranchers - or at least their foremen - know the whereabouts of their own cattle and can distinguish them from those of their neighbors if they want to. The West became cross-hatched with barbed-wire and steel posts. Even the engaging varieties of the old rail-fences largely disappeared except as ornamentation for the swank "ranchettes" of wealthy dudes. As a symbol, however, the maverick gained rather than lost prestige. Most of its popularity, like that of the "mustang," was only a reflection of the commercial exploitation of the mass itch for whatever gew-gaws would feed their lust for their plastic West and, consequently, was used as a catchy trade-name for anything from soap to soap opera - (my insincere apologies to the Ford Motor Company.) On a slightly more laudable level, it became associated with the futile, intellectually romantic resistance to the computerized culture of the mechanical bride and the automated groom.

For multiple reasons, wild horses were molested less relentlessly than wild cattle as they grazed the receding public lands. Horses were fleeter of foot. Before the dog-chow boom and the red-point panic accompanying the outbreak of the second world war, they were not in serious demand as food. The mustang also vanished from the range, however, and the wild horses that continued to avoid extermination in isolated areas were as undeserving of their glamorous name as was a long-eared weaner to the title, "maverick." Many of the last batch of "mustangs" rounded up by Fiddleback punchers on a 4th of July picnic wore forsaken brands. Nevertheless, the horse, wild or domesticated, has always been a more majestic symbol of freedom than the platter-destined cow. It would have been logical to expect "mustang" rather than "maverick" to become the distinctive appelation applied to independent, irrepressible individualists. Tracing irrational vicissitudes of language is occasionally informative. Mustangs travel in bands. The last of the resplendent mavericks travelled alone and evaded corrals, loading chutes, shipping-pens, ropes, reatas and hot-rods that composed the abject fate of the herd. The maverick became a scarce, solitary, furtive critter that glowered malevolently from the brush as circle-riders passed by unaware of its presence. It throve by exceptional ingenuity and hardihood. As the extent of the old spreads diminished and the land became scarred with the cankers of growth and "progress," the continued endurance of these old renegades confounds belief. When encountered, they proved themselves tough specimens of cunning, stamina and courage. In 1954 Clarence Genevo choked one down that had been loose in the Toiyabes for over four years. We called the mammoth Hercules. Clarence deserved the name too. Without assistance he'd brought him over ridges that bighorn sheep would have crossed mincingly and ran him into the main corral at the home-ranch where the animal put on a performance that would shame the fighting bulls of Andalusia.

"Want to put your rope on him, Doc?" Carl, whose sadistic humor never slept, had come out of the woodwork along with other members of the crew in anticipation of the chance to view a good side-show.

"Yeah," Zane added. "saddle up old Gizzard, you'll never get an easier chance for a little practice."

"Hind-foot him," Henry chimed in. "Clarence'll show you how and be there to back you if you miss a throw or two."

Better *not* miss," Jean called from the op'ra box, "I'm fresh outa shuck."

"Later," I said, eyeing the sullen critter standing like dynamite waiting for the fuse to reach the keg. "He's come a long way and looks wore out. I belong to the Humane Society. Wouldn't want to take unfair advantage."

"Guess you're right," Carl agreed amiable as the steer assembled himself for a frenzied charge at Wiggins who, at that moment, had the indiscretion to cut across the corral on foot with his milking-pails, "He sure looks wore down."

Hercules was not actually a maverick, but it is a technical irrelevancy. He was the stuff out of which real old-time mavericks were made. He wore a brand we hadn't used for four years. That was how we knew he had to be at least five years old. When one outfit buys out another it usually buys the cattle and whatever brands the sellers are running, thus avoiding possible future disputes. The mother cows would carry the old brands, the the new calves would be burned with the Fiddleback iron and the other brands phased out. Naturally, we concluded that Hercules had been branded by the former owner. He'd been at large a long time and our outfit never lost calves - except in those days he wouldn't have been considered "lost." No matter where he was found, Fairbanks or Timbuktu, his brand identified him.

Today, if you encounter a steer over four years old it's probably a dinosaur. It is no longer "economically profitable" to feed a steer for that length of time. The bigger he is, the more he consumes and the annual increment of additional weight diminishes. Consequently we eat immature, tasteless grain-fed beef so devoid of substance that any old gummer can chew it.

Mustangs are caught to be broken. There is nothing one can do with a maverick but butcher him or let him go his way. Buyers don't want him because he would not "grade evenly" with the rest of the bovine pygmies. And if he could be trucked and delivered to the Los Angeles stock-yards with minimal havoc, what then? He would bankrupt a feed-lot broker without adding marketable pounds. His grass-built T-bones would never fit the grills of suburban barbecue alchoholics, and quartered after a "dressed weight" shrinkage of seventy percent, he would still make four deep-freezes groan.

Thus it was the maverick, rather than the mustang, whose illustrious name was attached to the uncontained, self-sufficient iconoclast who refused to bend before the gale of society's "slave-morality" and acknowledged only the dictates of his own unconquerable spirit. As a stage in the process of civilization the frontier experience, like war and revolution, was a condition of social emergency. It required men of daring, decision, and endurance to cope with the challenges of ungrooved existence.

Flushing full-grown, undomesticated longhorns from the thornbush was only one of the activities that demanded brutal nerve, indifference to discomfort, hardship, pain, and even death. Men of the caliber of the great "mavericker" Shanghai Pierce, who built fortunes by unscrupulous vigor, were rarely docile when confronted by the drab, effete, monotonous restrictions of civil society. Wealth and age sobered some of them as grain and fenced pasture quiets the outlaw horse. Even Pierce became sufficiently tamed to adjust to a relatively conventional life. As for most of these men, they vanished like the mavericks they resembled, and organized society was quick to repudiate the code by which these dynamic argonauts of the plains had established their ascendancy. George M. Maverick's account of the true character of his father, together with the testimony of John Henry Brown, form a segment of civilization's conspiracy to destroy the ideology of the creative individualist. In reclaiming Sam Maverick from the fraternity of the Inspired Damned and reinstating him with the frock-coated babbitts of San Antonio's *Main Street,* in describing him as a man who "lived a life full of trusts and business . . . who died in the midst of his family," they render a service to fact and pay homage to decency, but they undermine a passionate legend. If I were Sam Maverick, fidgeting in my unquiet grave, I might prefer my myth to the truth. But Sam Maverick had elected to live under fence. Unless the kingdom beyond permits us to indulge sentiments that appear impermissible in this world, old Sam would probably have approved the efforts of his son to redeem his respectability and put in a plug for the virtues of the collar-and-hames cavvy.

The devil controls history and he has an obsession with ironic manipulation. Creative human beings possess the purpose, the dynamic energy and the integrity to produce the future which derives its strength from their efforts and then, when mature, uses that strength to destroy the values of its founders. Revolutions do indeed, like Saturn, devour their own children, but the granchildren devour the whole Revolution. Hegel explains the phenomenon with metaphysical profundity, but Ed Fisher could never be persuaded to read him. "Well," he reflected at the conclusion of one of my eulogies on the men and cultures of the past, "there's one edge we got on 'em."

"What's that," I asked.

"We're here and they ain't."

This brings us to the cream of civilization's jest. Settled in debilitating, easy-payment-plan comfort, the remnants of their shrunken minds transfixed by a square foot of jittering glass, the pitiable, spineless, sniveling, sycophantic slaves of the Gorgon-headed establishment revel in the antics of saddle tramps who are never gainfully employed, bonanza-ing rancheros whose fancy spreads miraculously operate themselves, and marshals who would be millionaires if paid by the corpse. Spellbound audiences thrill to the chivalry of noble mavericks who, single-handed or with the gamy assistance of a few loyal vassals, decide to empty a crooked gambling saloon, clean up a sin-infested town, rid the territory of sadistic outlaws—always upholding principle over expediency and reaffirming justice by direct action in the face of the grinding tyranny of a corrupt law and the apathetic gutlessness of an ossified community. These same audiences, fatuous and fragmented, return to their respective offices, practitioners as well as victims of the vices they had vicariously deplored and hissed the evening before. They have found their style of freedom - docile acceptance of imprisonment while remaining a cautious distance from all walls.

Throughout densely populated, suburban Squalidonia, the maverick is a hero as long as he confines his heroics to Stultavision, Blatherama and Disintigral Paperbacks, Inc. But whenever he is so indiscreet as to materialize and venture into the lush pastures of the current establishment, he is hazed off to forage with the wild cattle as quickly as possible. Like the Returning Savior in Ivan Karamazov's *Grand Inquisitor*, he is given the "bum's rush." Mavericks, when they show up at board meetings, political party caucuses, faculty convocations, legislative assemblies, or any of the numerous ritualistic, "deliberative" ceremonies contrived to give pseudo-liberal window dressing to the preordained policies of senile interest groups, are almost universally regarded as hotheaded villains—especially by those whom they are attempting to liberate. Rotten as the old corrals may be, they will hold as long as some on'ry critter can be prevented from taking it into his skull to give them a try. Such ambivalence, characteristic of the psychosis of nostalgia, betrays the confusion, self-deception, hypocrisy, and absurdity of homogenized establishmentarian society.

Present-day existence is hopelessly schizoid. Nobody *really* loves Big Brother, and inside the most timorous conformist a smothered rebel cringes in fear. The discrepancy between our ideals and daily realities is manifest in the fascination with which even intelligent people view western fantasies depicting the achievement of social justice by maverick heroes who rode roughshod over all obstacles and "put things right," and the silent despair most of us suffer at the shoddy compromises and degrading sell-outs we incessantly endure. How else is it possible to account for the fervid popularity of a novel and film such as *Shane*?"

Sophisticated critics insist that no mature person takes Westerns with their maverick heroes seriously—their popularity being attributable solely to their "escapist" entertainment value. It is a simple explanation that eliminates necessity for considering them critically and also allows one to enjoy them without admitting to complete infantilism. But the explanation is unconvincing. All childhood taste—especially that inspired by fairy tales and fables that are masterpieces of world literature—is not "infantile." Must concern for justice, truth, virtue be limited to pious hoosiers and naive bumpkins? Certainly the mature mind must be able to distinguish between fantasy and reality; and confronted with the present intellectually fashionable flight into the irrational and the epidemic of unintelligibility and nonsense, it is more important than ever to refuse to abandon the "ascertainable facts." Beyond demonstrable evidence and disciplined reason lies chaos. But ideals conceived from the union of reason and experience and tested in the crucibles of history are the standards by which civilization and culture are measurable. These ideals constitute a refined and reified type of historical fact which art assimilates, synthesises and expresses in inspirational form. Much western myth and legend can be described as "hokum" and its defenders contend that it is a hokum we cannot do without. The hokum does not consist of the inner nature of the myths and legends, but in their crude distortion. The ideals behind these myths were present long before the western frontier. The frontier provided another historical theater in which they could find expression. What elevates *Shane* to the status of literature is that the ideals retain plausibility and purity throughout the eminently human course of the action and do not cease to carry conviction under the impact of a conventionally dramatic plot structure. These same ideals remain valid even though the frontier has gone. The modern world presents challenges which, like all preceding epochs, requires heroes to meet them. Some literary pundits maintain that contemporary literature has discarded the concept of the hero because he no longer has "relevance." Only the "anti-hero" can accurately reflect life with honesty and integrity. Democracy, with its hostility to the notion of an elite, its deference to material values, its compulsion to perpetual compromise and expediency, has certainly made it tough on heroes in literature and in life. To have heroes it is necessary to have a code. A code is a set of principles which serve as the final justification of human actions. Without a code there are no guides to regulate human conduct except a compendium of capricious laws and the mass race for the trough. Expediency is not a code!

This is not a plea for a crusade, a demonstration of mock heroics or an assault upon the philosophy of expediency, but it does intend to call attention to the nemesis of self-deception. Palinurus was the pilot of Aeneas who jumped overboard because he could no longer endure Aeneas. The act was an attempt at dissociation with evil through self-immolation. It was also Virgil's vicarious atonement for his own servility before the power of Augustus for whose aggrandizement the poet had composed his iridescent but mediocre epic. What is the fate of court-poets in democracies? And why did Cyril Connolly, as the author of *The Unquiet Grave,* write under the name of Palinurus? And why did I bring the matter up at all and what has it got to do with the image of the *maverick* and the myth and reality of the cowboy and the lore and wisdom of the Fiddleback? For the present we will herd these critters into a holding spot and decide where to locate them later. It is sufficient to say that the maverick hero does not have to slay dragons, rescue priggish though comely school marms from runaways, hang rustlers, rout mortgage-shakers or gun-down Trampas at sun-down. All he has to do is disdain the race for the trough and differentiate between his guts and his belly.

This is the mark of the natural aristocrat and the clue to his superiority over the multitude. He is hated for it. But he is indifferent to vulgar opinion and appearances. Lancelot, bereft of his horse, journeyed to the lists at Camelot in a cart. The maverick possesses pride where others possess only vanity. When mavericks no longer appear among us, civilization is *kaputt.* With my nostalgia for the frontier, I yearn to see mavericks in high places. Yet the laws of societal selection and human gravitation seem to preclude the possibility that in the modern world a genuine maverick will ever attain a position of influence and power. No Shane is likely to become president, a university dean, or the chief executive of any establishment large or small. Let us not, for that reason, dispense with the dream. Mavericks will always be necessary. Even as losers.

Mustangs & Mustangers

"Hot damn, this is a larrupin' slab of prime beef," Henry exclaimed, pitching into the bounteous steak that sprawled across his plate. "Is it Fiddleback or one of John Casey's? It sure ain't one of them faded shad-bellies of yourn we been pounding ass all day bringing off that alkali grid."

"It's Safeway brand," Davy Stevens confessed, harpooning the rest from the smoking skillets and reloading them as the fat sputtered furiously. "Ain't no use me butchering. If you fellers weren't here it'd take me and Billy Jim most a year to eat up a beef - even if I gave all the guts and trimmings to the cats."

"Well," Zane scoffed. "I could polish off your top Diamond Hook steer before breakfast." He raked the last one onto his dish as Davy slapped a fresh platter of re-fills in front of him. There were seven of us, excluding Davy, wedged at the rectangular table that had been salvaged from a National Forest campground. With the attached side-benches, it took up most of the floor space of the combination messhouse and parlor that constituted one of the two rooms of Davy's false-brick shack at Cloverdale.

Henry shook his head in opposition to Zane's sarcastic exaggeration. "I couldn't," he said with mock-humility. "Not without I get me a set of them steel choppers they say the Rooskies can fit into a hand's jaw. The only tender part of Davy's steers is their feet."

Ed sat impassively at the head of the table in an imaginatively conceived custom-built chair made from the union of two empty lard tubs screwed together at their bases. Some of the staves of the top tub had been removed so that the intended occupant could back his posterior into the cavity thus formed. The cowhide tacked over the nesting section was frayed through to the wood like the sole of a worn out boot, but the chair's main shortcoming was that it had been constructed for Davy who was under five-feet "short." Ed, who had an eleven inch advantage over the old man, could not have been comfortable, but discomfort, physical or mental, never seemed to afflict our cowboss. He appeared at ease ensconced in Davy's gaddi except when building a smoke during the process of which he liked to tilt backwards, or hunch forward if we were camped in the open and he were sitting on a rock or a log. He'd finished eating and was probing for his tobacco. With the exception of breakfast, eating to Ed was not much more than a gesture. "Main trouble with your cows, Davy, is they're sand-logged. Every now and then they appreciate a little grass."

"Some of them animals did look a mite poor," Davy admitted reluctantly. He'd been preparing to dress down the "young whippersnappers," but Ed always "had him cowed when it came to the subject of cows," as Henry had once expressed it in one of his ebulliently witty moods. It was spring round-up and we were using Davy's isolated diggings as a line-camp. Billy Jim was his only hired help and since we shared overlapping range we had established a tradition of working our cattle together. Davy was over eighty. Only Emma knew his exact age and for reasons of her own, she kept it a secret. He would still put in a full day in the saddle between cooking our breakfasts and suppers while we did his chores. It was at Cloverdale that my dangerous milking talent leaked out. I'd been rash enough to win a bet. It cured me of gambling.

The seat at the opposite end of the table was a small wood-slatted folding-chair that had been filched from the Round Mountain School House. It was just right for Davy who hopped back and forth from stove to table like a perky sparrow, overly concerned that his guests lacked nothing. During a momentary lull in his culinary activity, he swung the chair around and straddled it. "Ain't been no moisture this end of the valley for two years," he complained in his shrill whinnying voice, "but when they get up in them hills in them green medders, you'll see a peck of difference. By fall them steers'll go eleven hundred or better."

Zane brayed and Henry nickered. "I'll bet my horse Tiger against that old '23 Moon you got stashed in your stone barn, that your goddam cows won't average eight hundred by October - even with the sand in 'em soaked up with water."

That's an even-money bet if I ever heard one," Zane said. "That fucking Tiger is about as much use as that goddam Moon. You might enter the sonova-bitch in the County Fair as something to scare away magpies."

"Shit, Zane," Henry said, considerably nettled, "what you know about horses wouldn't plug the hole left by an under-sized cattle-grub. That there Tiger is a full-blooded mustang. He don't look too purty, but he's all horse and he's got more bottom than your whole string shoved together."

"Mustang, my ass!" Zane exclaimed. "There ain't been a gen-u-wine mustang in this country for twenty years. And if he has so much bottom, how come you couldn't outrun them lead-assed steers I seed raring over Peavine this afternoon. When they come pouring off that ridge I knowed riders had to have stirred 'em up. And when I don't see no riders, I figgered it was you that fucked up and lost 'em. Me and Pinto brought 'em to heel before the ground-squirrels could reach their hole."

"When you run onto them steers they was so

plumb wore out anything could've caught up with 'em - even you and that pudding-footed Pinto."

"My old man run mustangs in Monitor, Antelope, Reese River and Frenchie's Flat right up through the war," Holly put in. "He'd sell 'em for horse meat when the army was grabbin' all the beef. I quit the old man about that time. I shore got kicks outa mustanging, but I never went fer chicken feedin' 'em. A feller's got no right to go eatin' horses." He chewed his mouthful of steak with gusto.

"There ain't nothing wrong with horse meat," Zane protested belligerently. "We 'et it all the time back home."

"I always suspected there was a warped-wheel in yer mormon upbringing," Jean muttered.

"I didn't say nothin' was wrong with horse meat," Holly fumbled apologetically for words, assuming Jean's caustic comment was directed at him. "I just meant it don't seem right for decent folk to eat it. You might as well go to eatin' people. And I ain't no Mormon."

"A fellow named Alfred Packer, one of Zane's countrymen, got to like it," I remarked.

"Horse meat or people meat?" Henry asked. "You don't always talk clear."

"Speaking of eatin' people reminds me of the time the cook at the old Y-Bench --" Jean began before I could reply, but Zane cut him off.

"Jeez, Holly, you're a dumb shit - talking about what's right to eat and what ain't. It's like Jean says," he pontificated also oblivious to the fact that he and not Holly had been the target of Jean's barb. "It's all what you was brought up to. Look at the injuns. They eat dogs, cats, jack-rabbits, ground squirrels. Hell, they even eat mules --"

Billy Jim scowled. "We don't eat no mules."

"Maybe not you Utes," Zane conceded, "but I know damned well 'Paches et mules. And them Navvies. *They* even et 'em alive."

"How the shit do you eat a mule alive?" Henry inflected his question with scorn and disgust. "You mean they et 'em raw."

"No, I mean they et 'em alive," Zane repeated emphatically. "When times was rough, they'd stake out a mule by their tee-pee, slice a chunk off its ass and cook it. Next day they'd slice a hunk off the other side and keep it up till the bastard was about dead. Then they'd finish it off - guts and all."

"Don't sound too larrupin' to me," Henry said scooping up another helping of frijoles. "I never did cotton to mules, but that's pretty unfriendly treatment. As fer eatin' dogs and cats, I can believe that. This here old chief was feedin' me real good once out at the Reservation. I'd et a lot worse tasting stuff and I asked him what it was and he told me it was duck. Sure didn't go down like duck so I asks him again. He kept saying 'duck' - 'good duck' - 'heap small duck.' Turned out later he'd been saying dog. But that weren't the worst part of it. When I rid up all these scrubby mutts come a-barkin' at me. There was this one cute little fart that took a shine to me and is following me around. It was just a pup and I went to pettin' him. The old squaw - well, she wasn't old - any injun gal over fifteen looks old - anyway she asked me if I liked the little dog. Naturally I said 'sure, he's cute.' So I got the little shitter for supper. Kee-rist!"

"It's a good thing it wasn't a mule's ass you was patting," Jean chuckled.

"I didn't think it was so funny," Henry said. "Damned near made me puke. Not so much from having et it, but for me being responsible for getting it killed. I was sorry for the poor little fucker. Anyway, I agree with Holly. A hand shouldn't ought to eat horses. Horses is too intelligent to eat."

Jean laughed again. "I've run afoul some dumb horses in my day and some blamed on'ry ones. But if brains is the reason fer not eatin' 'em, I never seen a horse as ignorant or on'ry as most people I've met up with. So maybe that Packer feller Doc mentioned had the right idea."

"Horses is a lot smarter than people," Holly chimed in. "Remember Crapper?"

"You mean old Croppy," Henry corrected.

"His name was Cropper all right," Holly agreed, "but you turds kept a-callin' him Crapper. So I finally give up. Now you pull a switch on me. A hand can't win around this outfit. Shove me them beans."

"There's plenty more in the pot," Davy said as Holly, hesitating and looking guilty, left a few lone drifters in the bowl.

"Anyhow —" With a decisive motion, he scraped the bowl clean, "if that there horse wasn't smart. He got the shakes one time somethin' awful. Not like Gus. Gus's got a habit of shakin' fer no reason. Scrambles your innards. This was somethin' different. I dunno what from. He'd maybe drunk bad water, or near foundered hisself stealin' oats, or et loco weed or bit into a wasp or somethin'. Anyways he got to shakin' holy bejeezus like a nigger swallerin' too heavy on gospel-grease. He was not good to ride acting crazy that way, so I unsaddles, turns him loose and fetches me another pony. For a long time after that he'd go to shakin' again whenever I threw the saddle on him. Oh, he'd let me saddle him all right - and even ride him a bit before he'd start them jitters. Had me plumb fooled fer a while. I finally figured he was just fakin' shakin' so I'd turn him loose - but I'd had me enough of that shit. I cinched the sonovabitch so tight he looked like a couple of linked sausages. Then I rode the shakes right out of him. He give up that trick, but he figured out a lot of other ones. Like every time I'd stop to bleed my lizzard —"

"They had this edjucated hoss at the Austin Rodeo last year," Henry interrupted. "Was he a smart sonovabitch! He'd carry messages to people, stand on his hind legs and beg, nod yes and no to questions on arithmetic, shake hands, take a handkerchief outa this here hand's pocket —"

"Circus tricks!" Jean spoke with derision. "That ain't what I call smart. Some sugar-peddling dude teaches 'em all them stunts. Now a real smart hoss is one that figures things out by hisself. I recollect a black-hearted, thieving gate-crasher we had at the old Y-Bench called Houdini. He'd open the barn door, help hisself to grain and shut it when he left. He'd break into the stack-yard, pull the outside bales off the corners and bust open the green ones. He'd let hisself out of the corral when you figured you'd locked him in fer keeps. He could locate every loose wire on the ranch and if he couldn't find one, he'd loosen some up and go through the fence without a scratch where an ordinary horse would of tore itself to tatters. Nobody learned him none of this. He done all the calculatin' without nobody giving him lessons." Jean flickered his eyelids nervously, a habit he had when he consciously began to think of something. "Least they didn't know they was giving 'em to him. One time I caught him eyeing me real careful, watching me open the gate into the West Field where the grass was sweet and thick and hadn't been tromped flat and stinking by the goddam cows. The cunning bastard was making notes on my moves and filing 'em away fer ref'rence. I rode into the buckbrush, left Whitey to graze and snuck back slow and quiet as a porcupine to watch what Houdini done next. Sure as thorns in the beds in hell, no sooner was I out of sight than he'd pranced over and set to work on that there gate —"

"No horse can open them Australian gates," Zane declared. "I don't give a shit how smart he is."

"When it comes to smart horses," Henry plunged in, taking advantage of Zane's interruption, "I was reading a story by Will James about a blind cowhand. The horse done about everything for him. The story ended with this here horse tip-toeing acrost the ties on a washed out railroad trestle with this blind hand on his back. It was during a flood. The horse saved the train —"

"That's a crock of shit," Zane objected. "A blind cowhand, my ass! I suppose the horse done the ropin'?

Did it dally or tie hard-and-fast?"

"The story didn't go into that part," Henry said. "But there was another story I read about a horse that saved a little girl that was lost on the range. This horse was a mustang stallion. He picked up this little shitter with his teeth and plunked her on the back of a mare that was too big for her to climb by herself and whipped 'em off home to her folk's ranch."

"How the hell'd he do that?" Zane wanted to know, his tone registering contemptuous disbelief. "How'd the horse know which ranch she come from? How'd he inform the goddam mare where to go?"

"Well," Henry mused, "best I kin remember, this here stud knew all the ranches in them parts. He'd looked 'em over from time to time and run off the mares he wanted. The mare he set this little old girl on was one he'd led off from her father's spread. If you read the story, it explains it all clear."

"I'll bet," Jean haw-hawed, slapping his thigh.

"Horses has done some pretty smart things in their day," Henry continued unabashed. "People have writ a lot about them - mostly people what don't know much and go in fer a deal of hearsay and exaggeratin'. I been around the critters all my life and I reckon I oughta try my hand at writin' a really honest-to-god horse yarn."

"Being around horses don't mean you can write about em," Zane said. "You gotta have some know-how about puttin' a story together so's it makes sense. You got to have a shit-pot full of fancy words, too —"

"I ain't so sure it's all that tough," Henry countered. "You just got to have some characters and have somethin' happen."

"I'd write me about old Crapper." Holly said. "Somep'n was a happenin' with him ev'ry time I got on him. I remember leadin' him off the top of Jefferson when he wheeled around on me and started fallin' off that goddam cliff - backwards —"

"Speaking of cliffs," Henry said, "I figgered to build me a story about this here famous mustang stallion named Blue Fucker. He was born an orphan on accounta his pappy - a big black wild-assed stud - had run his whole band of mares over this here cliff to escape being caught by a bunch of shit-brained mustangers. His mother was a white roan."

Zane winced. "What in hell is a white roan?"

"Same as a red roan or a blue roan exceptin' it's white." Henry swung his legs over the bench and began to buck his dishes. The room was hot. Frenzied moths kept slamming into the kerosene lamp and falling onto the empty plates where they fluttered and floundered helplessly, their wings trapped in smears of grease and ketchup.

"Leave them dishes set or you'll start a traffic jam," Davy said. "I'll clean this mess up after you boys bed down."

"You should saw these benches free and push the table against the wall when you ain't using it," Ed advised, "you'd have more room and everybody could spread out his legs."

"It's only crowded like this when you fellers are here," Davy explained. "The rest of the year there's only me and Billy Jim and most of the time he ain't here neither."

"All the better reason to saw these damn benches off," Ed insisted. "You only need one edge of the table and your chair for yourself. You can move the benches onto the porch and we can carry them in when we need 'em."

"What I can't figure out is how Davy got this damned tourist fixture in here in the first place," I said. "There's only two doors and you'd have an awkward time hauling a saddle through either of 'em."

Ed scratched at his forehead and eased out a slow, languid drawl. "Well, come to think of it Doc, you've raised a mighty tantalizing problem. If it was you, how'd you go about getting the thing inside without tearing out a wall?"

"Well, I guess I'd have to take it apart."

"Doc, you're a genius."

"We could dress like Santa Claus and pack it down the chimney," Zane suggested helpfully.

"There ain't no chimneys if you don't count that old stove-pipe," Holly pointed out.

"You fellers are brewing up a problem where there ain't none." Henry had settled himself onto a small stump of juniper he'd pulled out of the woodbox. "You just set the table up first and build this shack around it. I admit it's a hard way to do it, it'd take most of an afternoon. Anyways, my mare's name was —"

"It's all put together with bolts," Davy said. "It would of had to be took apart to get it in so I done it up at the campground so it'd be easier to load in the pick-up. I didn't have nobody to help out and I didn't aim to try lifting it by myself. Loosening them bolts was bad enough. They was rusted on pretty tight."

"Goat-pussy!" Henry snorted.

"Goat-Pussy?" Jean repeated. "That's some handle for you to hang on a horse being you're so all-fired particular."

"Kewpie - Tiger -" Zane sneered in a mock-whimper.

"Goat-Pussy wasn't her name," Henry complained impatiently. "I was just cussing out my disgust at you bastards for always interrupting my story. The mare's name was —"

"If it was a wild mare it wouldn't of had no name," Zane stated flatly.

"This mare hadn't always been wild," Henry explained. "It was a purebred Ay-rab that had vamoosed from the stable of an English lord when it was a yearling —"

"This is startin' out one helluva story," Jean sniggered. "I sure don't see no English lord naming his purebred Ay-rab, Goat-Pussy."

"I already said it's name wasn't Goat-Pussy," Henry persisted stubbornly, "it was Silver Queen —"

"Sounds like the name of a mine," Zane said.

"Do you bastards want to hear this story or not?"

"Let's hear it fer chrissakes!" Holly begged.

"Okay! Goat-Pussy had busted all four legs when she went off that rim-rock and couldn't run or get up or nothin' but she went ahead and dropped this here little horse-colt. That little shitter managed to suck before his poor ma died in terrible agony. This give him enough steam to wobble around over this awful pile of dead and groaning mustangs. It was a horrible sight. It woulda made the stoutest hand shudder to set eyes on it. Worse'n some gruesome massacree. Worse'n the morning after Custer's Last Stand —"

"You must have watched those Nazi-death camp films too late at night," I intruded impulsively.

Ed Fisher ran his fingers through his hair and frowned. "You're drifting pretty far from water, Henry. Don't know where you aim to peddle this yarn, but even citified folk will choke at a mare with four broken legs throwing a colt, cleaning it up and squirming into a position for it to suck."

"How come you have to bust four legs? One'd be plenty," Zane said.

"That wouldn't help none," Jean jeered. "Your troubles ain't even begun. You're gonna have to do some fancy explaining to raise that colt without no mother."

"You guys are forgettin' about them rustlers," Henry said.

"Rustlers? What rustlers?" several voices inquired almost in unison.

"I mean them mustangers. They finally come up with the band after it had poured itself over that there ledge. They stand lookin' over the mass of writhin' corpses - sort of sick like. It got to 'em. Some of 'em even took vows never to run mustangs again. Then they turn and head back fer the ranch. All but this greaser, Pancho. Pancho Gonzales. Pancho spots the little shitter down there and decides to rescue him."

"Ed made a point back there," Jean interposed. "It'd square your yarn up a mite if your Good Samaritan wet-back was to find the mare dyin' in the throes of motherhood and gets Green Fucker out by cutting her open —"

"Blue Fucker," Henry corrected. "But come off it, Jean! Nobody - and I mean *nobody'd* believe your way of tellin it. You don't give horses scisserians. Least I never heard of it."

"Don't see why that should stop you," Jean grumbled. "You ain't got nothin' in your goddam story yet that anybody ever heard of. And while we're at it, where in blazes was that there English lord's stable located at? Did your crazy mare swim the Atlantic Ocean?"

"Okay," Zane interrupted impatiently, anxious to bring the story to an end, "Let's allow the Mex adopts your stoopid colt. I suppose he brings it up on a bottle. Filled with Tequila."

"Tequila and sheep's milk," Henry modified. "It's a formula. But first he had to have the colt baptised."

"Baptised!" It was a chorus of inharmonious indignation.

"Yessir! And christened."

"That must've been some performance," Jean said. "I can see the priest splashing on that there holy water and sayin' 'I hereby tag thee Blue Fucker in the name of Father, Son and Holy Ghost."

"No, no!" Henry protested. "He didn't get *christened* Blue Fucker. He didn't latch on to that name till later - when he went to runnin' wild, got hisself a terrific *manada* and started throwing colts all over the range."

"I'm shore relieved to hear that," Jean sighed. "It

would've been a christening that emptied the church. So what name do they baptise him with?"

"Jesus," Henry pronounced solemnly.

"Jeezus H. Christ!" Holly exclaimed, "That's a helluva name fer a hoss. Blue Fucker's bad enough. But - Jeezus, Holy Shit!"

"All right, you guys," Zane growled, "Lay off. You're carrying it too far. Have some respect, for chrissakes. You sound like a bunch of fucking atheists."

"What in hell's eatin' you?" Henry wanted to know. "What you suddenly gettin' so goddam pious about?"

"Nothin's eatin' me," Zane replied. "You just don't go around calling some sonovabitching horse, Jesus. It's sacreligious."

"Who said Brown Fucker was a sonovabitching horse?"

"Blue Fucker," Jean corrected. "Ain't you fergettin'?"

"Blue Fucker," Henry acknowledged. "He was a damn good horse. Plenty of bottom and as smart as a keg of dictionaries."

"I don't give a shit how smart the horse was," Zane said, "You don't have to go around calling him Jesus."

"I ain't going around calling him Jesus," Henry said. "That's what this here Mexican feller called him."

"Yeah, but you're making up the goddam story," Zane insisted with considerable heat.

"If you'd a-been around a-tall," Henry persisted,

ignoring Zane's logic, "you'd know Jesus is a perfectly okay name in May-hikko. Mexies all names their kids Jesus. I used to play with a little greaser named Jesus Gomez. And there was Jesus Otero and a Jesus Pulque —"

"Christ," Jean interrupted, "finish your rat-brained story! We can't sit up all night. What happens after the wet-back christens the Blue Fucker Jesus?"

"Well," Henry continued, feigning injured feelings and proceeding as if reluctant to squander his pearls, "he was a real gentle horse. This here Pablo Gonzales figgered to make a racer out of him because he could move faster'n a striped-assed ape. Everything was a-going fine. He'd worked him out quite a bit —" Henry paused and scratched his head thoughtfully. "I'm gonna have to skip some here till the horse grows up. There was a lot happened in between. When he was just a yearlin' —"

"If yer gonna skip, skip fer chrissakes," Jean blurted irritably.

"Okay," Henry yielded. "But some of this is important to savvying what come later. Fr'instance, there was a ranch hand working fer Pancho. They'd had a set-to and Pancho had run him off the place. Spades - that was this here hombre's name - Ace Spades, they called him - Well, Ace swore he was gonna get even with Pancho if it took him the rest of his life —"

"So Ace Spades sneaks back one night and steals Blue Fucker," Jean volunteered.

"Jeezus," Henry exclaimed in astonishment, "How'd you figger it?"

"You changing the horse's name back, or just cussin'?" Zane asked.

"Seems maybe I heard this story somewheres before," Jean grumbled.

"Not this story," Henry maintained with pride. "Hell, I ain't even made it all up yet. Couldn't tell ya how it comes out myself."

"What happens after that Ace feller stoled the horse?" Holly asked eagerly.

"That's easy to figure," Zane volunteered. "Spades is a mean sonovabitch. He beats the shit out of the horse every day until there come a time when Jesus - that's still a helluva name for a horse —" he muttered paranthetically, "turns killer. He rears up and tramples Spades to death, busts outa the corral and joins up with the outlaw horses."

"Any you boys fer dee'zert?" Davy inquired. "I built us a boggy-top. Ran short on raisins and finished her off with prunès. Don't reckon it'll kill nobody." He circulated the table wielding a spatula over the pie-skillet.

"Goddam," Henry complained testily. "Who's makin up this here story anyhow?" He shook his head disgustedly. "But that's about what happened, all right. Zane just left out the best part - about this here cowhand, Shorty. He's a ex-rodeo champ and a real flash-forker when it come to savvying horses. Seems he'd won Jesus off Pablo in a poker game about the time Spades stoled him. So the joke is on Spades, after all."

"Somehows, that don't dredge no laughs - least fer me it don't," Jean remarked with a quizzical expression on his dour face.

"It ain't meant to be funny like a cripple bustin' his crutch," Henry hastened to explain. "Spades was out to get revenge on Pablo, but Pablo don't own the horse no more. Get it?"

"Yeah, yeah," Jean said. It's complicating your story without adding much point though."

"It don't matter none cause Pancho's out of the deal from now on anyway." Henry went on, "Meantime, Shorty had cottoned on to Jesus, who he'd renamed Pard. Him and Pard get to be real buddies and Shorty's shook up bad when Pard turns up missing from the corral. Now comes a long part where Shorty sets to trackin' down Spades. Every time he's about to ketch up with him something happens and old Ace gets away. If you fellers want to hear —"

"You kin skip that part," Jean obligingly conceded. "You're a-tangled enough in yore own rope already."

"How you mean?" Henry demanded.

"I ain't no hand at yarn-spinnin'," Jean said, "but you claim Shorty just won Jesus in a poker game when he was stoled. Then it turns out he's been palin' around with the horse a long spell and has re-named him Pard. There's too many kinks to my mind —"

"That can be easy straightened out," Henry said. "Sure, Shorty has knowed Pard a long time. He just ain't *owned* him. He's wanted to buy him off'n Pancho, but Pancho won't sell. That's why he's got to win him gamblin'."

"I don't like callin' the horse Pard," Holly complained. That's the name of a dog food. It —"

"Anyways, you got too many hands in the story," Jean persisted. "Why'd you have to bring this Shorty feller into it? Why don't you have Shorty raisin' Pard in the first place? Then you could dump Pancho, or Pablo, or whatever his goddam name was, altogether. You wouldn't have to make folks mad calling the horse Jesus and keep changing his name all the time. It's confusin'."

"I got reasons," Henry answered. "I just didn't want to take a lot of time going into 'em. I figgered whoever was followin' the story would allow that I knowed what I was doin' without havin' to spell it all out. If I was bringing in a bunch of steers, Ed would be satisfied just to see me deliver 'em to the corral. He wouldn't ask fer no account of every rock, bush and gully I steered 'em around along the way." He shook his head in weary disappointment at the distrust of his fellow man. "I didn't want Shorty mixed up in running them mustangs over the cliff. He's too nice a feller. It was okay for a Mexican. But I didn't want no greaser owning my horse fer keeps. Pablo was all right fer startin' out with. In real life, horses picks up all sorts of different names depending on what different folks owns 'em. No two people cotton to the same names. Look at the objections you guys raised. And what about Doc's horse, Brown Pisser? - which incidentally give me the idea of naming my stud, Blue Fucker - them little girls who used to own him called him old Star. . . I guess I'll just have to go into all this when I write it up. There's probably a lot of readers as dumb as you hands. Jeezus! Right now, I don't know if I got the bottom for it. I figgered I was running this here story right down a slick groove —"

"What happens when Shorty ketches the horse thief?" Holly, indifferent to the literary subtleties, demanded with the petulance of a kid being deprived of his candy-cane.

"Shorty tracks him down," Henry plunged on with renewed zeal, encouraged by Holly's uncritical interest, "but he don't get there till Pard has stomped him and taken off. Remember? All he finds is a dead body in the corral."

"Cold fingers clutching the Ace of Spades," Ed added.

"Ya know what'd make a helluva part in your story?" Holly interrupted with a burst of enthusiasm. "Pard finds this band of mustangs blastin' about on this here mesa. It's led by a big black stallion named Thunder. Pard and Thunder square off and you could have a real rip-snortin' battle where they rear up, scream and paw the dust until Pard, all bloody and pantin' whips Thunder outa the band and runs him off —"

"You better have that there Pard knock around a year to two so's he kin take on a little muscle and edjacashun'," Jean warned. "No two year old is gonna whip no stud with a bunch of mares - no matter what age your goddam Thunder's packin'!"

"I'd figgered on that," Henry said. "If you gents would take a couple of half-hitches on your jaws long enough fer me to tell it. I was aimin' to have Pard take on Thunder - only I was gonna call him Lightning and make him all white. Anyways, Pard takes on Lightning, gets whipped and ducks out. Remember, he could run like three hens dodging Emma's axe. This fight teaches him plenty. He grub-lines it fer a coupla winters and gets really fleshed out and toughened up. When he runs up agin' Lightning in the spring, he's wise to the old fart's tricks and this time he takes him."

"What happened to Shorty?" Davy inquired, loading plates into a washtub. "He seemed a decent sort of feller."

"I was coming to him," Henry said. "Shorty had been working around a lot of ranches. Every now and then while ridin' line and wintering the herd he'd ketch a glimpse of Pard, but never could get close to him. Pard had grown too smart for any man. Shorty saves up, gets a little spread of his own, marries a school teacher and sets about raisin' a family. He's got a station wagon, a small bunch of cows and some good brood mares. He's makin' out okay when —"

"You oughta not have Shorty git married," Holly implored. "And what does he want with a goddam station wagon?" His dismay at the turn Henry's tale was taking was poignant.

"What you got agin' marryin'?" Henry asked. "Only this mornin' you was talking about hookin' up with Buck Yancey's apple-assed tomato. If that ever gets around, we'll be pickin' you off a cottonwood limb."

Holly, momentarily routed, retreated into humble silence. Jean came to his rescue. "Holly's right. It ain't gonna help yer yarn none to fix Shorty in a double-harness and tie him down with a ranch and a flock of kids. When I owned my ranch I didn't have time to shit comfortably. If he's ever gonna drop a loop on that outlaw horse, you're a-better off keepin' him a lone coyote."

"I'd counted on Shorty maybe trying to corral one of Blue Fucker's colts fer his kid fer Christmas," Henry said defensively.

"Look" Zane cut in, "This Shorty's gonna be your main hand. Right? Then he ought to be the sort who amounts to something instead of just some saddle-bum. I'd give him a ranch and hook him up with a slick looking broad - one with class. Then throw in three or four tow-headed kids."

Henry rubbed his chin thoughtfully. Zane's argument seemed to fortify him with negative conviction. "Yep," he said, watching the moths dashing against the lamp, "we can't give him no wife and kids. And the hell with the station wagon. Come to think of it, every time I see some horse-pitcher, the top johnny and his squaw is always barreling around in a station wagon. Maybe I been influenced some. We'll keep this hand unfenced. He can be a guy some open-heifer threw over before the story begins. So he wanders around working different outfits, bustin' broncs and ridin' rough string when he's not hittin' the circuit. Maybe he's eyin' Lightning with the idea of enterin' him in rodeo. Yeah! That's it!" he exclaimed, his face brightened with animation.

"Keep rodeo out of it, or you'll stray from the range," Jean advised.

"Blue Fucker! He's really earning his name now," Henry proceeded to take off like fire in the wind. "The ranchers give it to him because he's littering the entire west with galloping colts. Shorty's getting more and more hung up on this horse. He's got to have him. Plumb crazy-like. But Blue Fucker keeps eludin' him. Shorty tries running and roping him, but he can't get no horse fast enough to keep up with him. Next, he tries trappin' him, but Blue Fucker's always too smart. He even thinks of creasin' him, but that's too risky. Too many good horses has got'n kilt that way no matter how fair a shot a hand is —"

"He should have wrapped a hunk of burlap around his foot and hobbled out onto the mesa and the whole miserable band would have come after him," Jean said, "like the time the remuda took after Holly thinking his foot was a feed-bag."

"You can't ketch no wild horse with oats," Holly declared, his attention temporarily redeemed from contemplating the filly tending the Round Mountain grocery counter and restored to the range.

"Shorty tried everything," Henry continued. "That horse was too much for man or beast and wasn't of no mind to be corralled."

There was a long pause. Whether from suspense or boredom, it was difficult to tell, but everyone seemed to have run out of comments. Ed slowly rolled himself another smoke. Jean walked wearily to the stove and poured himself a mug of fresh coffee from the chipped blue porcelain-plated pot.

"Fill me up while you're on your feet, Jean," Zane said, looking gloomy. Jean filled Zane's cup and made the rounds. Davy was replacing cooking utensils on the hooks on the bare plank walls. "There's plenty more of this prune puddin'," he offered.

Holly accepted. There were no other takers.

Henry sat with his lips pursed, pondering the worn spots and coffee stains that had left intricate designs on the unmatched pair of oil-cloth table covers. Holly scratched his backside and, unable to contain himself longer, inquired through a bulging mouthful, "What you waitin' on, Henry? How'd Shorty finally ketch that there mustang?"

Henry raked his head in desperation. "I ain't actually figgered that out yet. Fact I don't know if he oughta ketch the horse a-tall."

"You got to have him catch the fucking horse," Zane expostulated, emerging from a temporary state of moody silence, "otherwise your goddam story won't make no sense. The hero has got to get what he's going after, else he ain't much of a hand."

"Shorty ain't the hero of my story," Henry said. "Blue Fucker is. I don't want the sonovabitch caught. Unless I was the one doing the catching. That might make a difference."

Jean laughed with good humored scorn. "It don't matter who ketches him - or if nobody ketches him," he joshed, "but you still got to have an end to yer story, else you brung us all out here onto the salt flats fer nothin'."

"I figgered I might have him get kilt - or disappear," Henry mused. "Nobody'd really a-knowed what become of him. His ghost could go prancing anywheres he pleased. On moonlight nights he'd keep showin' up at different places from Sonora to Saskatchewan. I'd call the story, *The Phantom Stud.*"

"You oughta kill off all the crazy sonsabitches,

Shorty, Pablo and Blue Fucker," Jean announced. "Ain't none of yer characters worth keepin' around - even fer laughs. If Blue Fucker was caught, he wouldn't be worth a shit to nobody. He'd allus be snappin' ropes or tryin' to kick the be-jeezus outa you every time you clumb in or out of the saddle. As fer that Shorty, if he's too fucking stoopid to ketch a goddam ignerant mustang, he ain't worth his feed —"

"I tole you this was a damn smart horse," Henry said with rising feeling. "There weren't no man good enough to ketch him."

"I ketch him." Billy Jim grunted.

Henry, Holly and Zane all stared at Billy Jim with a mixture of horror and stupefaction. After a stunned pause, they all began to speak at once.

Zane: "What the hell do you mean, you'd ketch him?"

Holly: "How'd you go about it?"

Henry: "You'd never lay a rope on Blue Fucker! Ain't I made it clear? He was too slick."

"I'd ketch me that horse," Billy Jim repeated.

Henry was exasperated. "Look, I ain't sayin' you ain't a pretty good hand, but I thunk up this here story and I'm sayin' nobody - and I mean *nobody* - no goddam injun or nothin' is gonna ketch my horse!"

" Story no good," Billy Jim growled, waving his arm brusquely. "I'd ketch me that horse." He got up and fought his way into his alpaca army jacket. "Going to bunkhouse. Bum story. Good only to make man sleepy." He slapped his brightly banded, battered stetson on his black, squat pumpkin-shaped head and stalked out of the shack.

There was a prolonged and somewhat awkward silence while everyone sipped half cold coffee. Finally Zane blurted, "What in Christ's name did that fucking indian mean, "I'd ketch me that horse. "?"

"He meant he'd catch the horse," Ed said with a faint smile.

"You know what I mean," Zane continued with vexation. "I mean how the hell did he aim to do it? That's all I want to know. Christ! I've ridden with that dead-assed bastard. He's slower than an over-stuffed possum. He couldn't catch a three-legged porcupine trying to cross an acre of fallen logs. Let alone that there mustang."

"You was the one wanted Blue Fucker caught," Holly reminded him. "You musta had some idea how it was gonna be done. Maybe Billy Jim had figgered out a way."

"Billy Jim was right," Jean said. "There ain't no horse a man can't ketch provided he goes about it right. Them full-stamped mustang yarns is all a crock of shit. I ain't arguing that there weren't horses that could give an ordinary hand a run fer his money. But the only reason they wasn't caught was that the hombres a-chasin' them fucked up somewhere's along the line. They either run 'em over cliffs like you had them crazy fools do in the start of yer story - or they run 'em to death - or got 'em trompled and crippled in corrals that was too small. About all they accomplished was to orphan a fine stand of colts. Whatever they done wrong, it was either no brains, no guts, no patience - and probably all three. But that goddam injun Zane thinks is so slow would of just ambled after that mustang stud day after day until yer goddam Blue Fucker was too plumb wore out to flick flies off his own ass. Shit, he'd git so he'd take fright the minute he smelt that creepin' red-skin a-comin'. Most white men ain't got that kind of stickability. They'd be like Zane - in a big damn hurry to get back to his dog-pecker pink cadillac and the cut-rate cunts in town."

"If I had nothing better to do than an illiterate injun," Zane said, "maybe I would blow twenty years trying to run down the sonovabitch. But that's the whole point. An ass-hole that throws away half his life chasing some no-good horse has got loose gravel for brains."

"What pisses me off," Henry complained, "I'd bet my rig and bed-roll that Billy Jim couldn't of caught Blue Fucker. In spite of what Jean says." He turned appealingly to Ed. "What do you think, Ed?"

"Remember your three queens," Ed said.

"That ain't no answer. You know what I mean, Ed. Could Billy Jim of caught that horse?"

Ed Fisher sighed, grinned and took a frustrating length of time to reply. "Well," he said, releasing his words leisurely, "I'm not rightly certain which goose will make it south for the winter and which one will make it into Emma's oven. I've known hands who couldn't drive a nail into a bale of hay - and I've known horses that made a streak of lightning look like it was part of a funeral procession - and I guess that's the sort of animal you've got in mind for your Cobalt Casanova —"

Henry frowned. "Come on, Ed, quit bellying through the brush."

"If I were putting money on it I'd want that fourth queen and I'd want 'em made out of aces." He placed the palm of his hand on the table, "I'd lay my roll on Billy Jim."

ii

By the end of the week we had gathered the Fiddleback and Diamond Hook stock and commenced parting them out. Henry's (or Will James') blind cowhand could have done it. It wasn't necessary to be able to read a brand or an ear-mark. Zane suggested we just run 'em around the pasture for a few minutes. The Fiddlebacks would be on their feet, fat and sassy, and could be herded out the gate and Davy's left in the field.

"Yeah," Henry added, "but it'll bust our guts tailing 'em up."

Hell! My saddle is slipping. I'm getting my books mixed up. This stuff belongs in *The Leather Throne.* We better head back for the wagon while it's light enough to stay on the trail. . .

the Cowboss

We topped the divide separating the sage-flecked swells of upper Reese River basin from the furrowed eastern scarp of the Toiyabes. Asserting common-law rights, our horses stopped of their own accord after the steep rapid climb, blew gustily against their cinches, lowered their heads and settled into hip-shot immobility. Jean Daniels rolled a smoke and, faithful to the pace of conversation on the range, began building his answer to the question I had put to him an hour before. "Tying onto the cowboss is like roping a special bronc you've fixed your eye on out of a band of on'ry mustangs. Others'll upstage him and draw your bead off target. They'll get in the way when you're shaking out your loop. Making the ketch takes more patience and luck than fancy hemp-tossing." Jean's eyes never stopped scanning the mohagany strewn ridges and confluent aspen-choked ravines that sloped with rugged grace into the adjacent watersheds. "You ain't gonna make it without wasting some throws. Fact is you probably ain't gonna make it anyways."

Well - I've wasted several throws in clumsy attempts to tie down the cowboss. When I turned the subject toward Jean, who had the reputation of being able to rope a lizard from a crack in a rock or a cat off the limb of a pine-tree (I'm not referring to household pets), I thought if he could hind-foot him I might swing a Mother Hubbard on his head. Maybe the best approach is to settle for watching him a spell in open pasture.

Cowboss is not listed in Ramon Adams' near-definitive glossary of cow-camp lingo. Neither is it to be found in Peter Watts' *Dictionary of the Old West* nor in Denis McLaughlin's encyclopedia covering the same terrain. In accounts of the cattle frontier, trail bosses, wagon bosses and range bosses crop up thicker than the left-overs in Wiggins' goulash, but these terms were discarded by cowmen when conditions that produced them melted into the past. The cowboss was the legitimate heir to their legacy. "Foreman" and much worse, "ramrod," are titles almost always misapplied by fiction writers to characters performing the functions of the cowboss, or what is a variant of the same sinful error, characters cast in a role that should have belonged to a cowboss are made to engage in activities a working cowboss would shun. In range metaphor, these candidates for stardom had been "saddled with a dead horse." During protracted association with outfits that had not "went dude" I never heard a full-rigged, nickel-plated buckaroo refer to the cowboss as a foremen or a ramrod. Novelists ignorant of ranching operations that were other than stage-sets and intent upon diverting their protagonist's attention to saloons and gun-play, have kept the existence of cowbosses a secret. But those hand-hewn personalities active in the days before running cows was replaced by "raising cattle," were truly the models for *The Last Cavalier*. The exit of the cowboss lacked the theatrical mystique of Remington's melodramatic ikon, but a herd of longhorns could have been hazed through the gap his departure left in western traditions.

A frenzy of experts will paw their own dust over most of what follows. I used to respect authorities until a contemporary dictionary cost me a bet with an untutored ignoramus by defining "feel" as "to *think*." No cowhand ever played me this false. With his customary trenchancy, Jean Daniels defined a cowboss as "the feller in the outfit who packs a spare set of guts and is long enough on savvy to leave 'em strung on the fence when they ain't needed."

Critters with slow-brands have been cut back from this discourse. Accepted misuses of terms have been rejected in order to portray the cowboss as he was to the men who rode with him, and to preserve unpolluted the essence of those qualities that render him worthy of chaste immortality. If he had not chosen to secede from the human race, Jean Daniels would have made a *great* cowboss. But he lost his small ranch to "the banks" during the Behemoth of depressions and it soured him on conventional ambition. From then on he never pastured a dollar and ignored his wages except when he ran out of whiskey. Late in life he inherited a sizeable stake and got rid of it like he was spitting out a wasp. Ed Fisher was one of the few men who could decoy a clear-footed opinion from him. If a book-wrangler forking his roll-top and twirling his tally-sheets were to ask him if he thought a batch of steers were ready for shipping, Jean would reply, "Why doncha ask 'em?"

Let's tighten the cinches and get down to cases.

ii

> "Consider Charterhouse to speak for me on any occasion when I am not personally with you," said Old John Nickum, facing the assembled Box M riders. "When he gives an order, you are to obey it without qualification. Is that clearly understood? From now on he is my right hand man."

Confronted with this slack-mouthed introduction by which a seasoned composer of horse-opera, Ernest Haycox, depicted a presumably experienced cattleman presenting a new cowboss to the crew, even a company-curried cowhand as servile as Owen Wister's Virginian would have cringed like a wise dog cornered with an incensed skunk. Old John's rash harangue would have turned the Box M into a ghost ranch. In their own laconic vernacular, the disgusted hands would have "punched the breeze." Had Old John made the right choice in naming a cowboss, Clint Charterhouse would have spurned the dead horse Haycox betrayed Old John into saddling for him, cleaned the mud clogging the arrogant rancher's plow and led the boys over the ridge himself.

Charterhouse, despite his stereotyped virile virtues, was not the man for the *job.* He was the mysterious stranger riding into a stock-company frontier town. He did not know the country. He did not know the cowhands and they did not know him. He knew cattle, but he did not know the Box M cows. A cow to the uninitiated may seem analogous to one of ex-Governor Reagan's redwoods, but to know one is not to know them all. Charterhouse had demonstrated lightning speed and lethal accuracy with his Colt 45. And he had, of course, met the rancher's daughter. Although a prime specimen of a catalog hero for a thud-and-blunder western, as head nurse for several thousand longhorns, Charterhouse's accomplishments were trivial.

A cowboss was not a trouble-shooting chuck-line rider skilled in prosaic forms of violence which he chivalrously placed at the disposal of assorted losers. A cowboss had no time for frivolous adventures rescuing comely widows and orphaned daughters from the clutches of unscrupulous mortgage holders and corrupt foremen. He was too busy producing the calf-crop that would eventually service the mortgage payments. He was vigilantly patrolling the range so that losses to wolves, cats, weather, sod-busters and other busy predators were minimal. He frequented saloons about as often as he attended church. He avoided settlements as if they were plague-ridden and never bought chips in the burgher's promotional schemes. He left townspeople to fight municipal peculation by themselves with the pea-shooters of law and democratic politics. He saved his six-gun for crippled livestock and tomato cans. He rarely wasted ammunition popping heads off rattlesnakes which are harmless if left alone and far less dangerous than one's fellow man.

Running any spread larger than a shirt-tail operation required the cowboss to spend more time in dry-camps (hoping they'd stay that way, but knowing they wouldn't) using the clean earth for a mattress than nesting in bunk-house straw. He knew the country by sections and townships more intimately than the churlish homesteader knew his squalid holdings and, if given his forty acres would have lost his mule in it. Possessing the ever-lively curiosity of a coyote, a memory that could store whatever he observed and a natural faculty for uncanny logic, the cowboss' unerring judgments often made ordinary hands suspect him of an infallibility endowed by the devil. I recall an instance when Ed Fisher invited me to accompany him tracking a stray that had taken advantage of a drift-gate indifferently left open by some incompleat angler. Before we had gone very far Ed remarked casually, "It's a three-year old steer."

"How do you figure that?" I inflected my tone

with irreverent skepticism to make certain that he'd realize I was unimpressed.

"Size, shape and depth of the hoof prints."

"Yeah. But a *steer* . . .?"

"A steer walks different. Besides, if it were a cow there'd be calf tracks following her."

We progressed up the canyon another quarter of a mile in silence. "She could be a dry cow."

Ed laughed. "You been thinkin'." Another short laugh.

"Well?"

"Well she ain't!" He condescended to explain. "All our dries are down below on BLM range."

"Maybe she left her calf bedded down someplace while she went to water." I was determined to indicate that I was not completely ignorant of the habits of our charges.

"Not likely," Ed explained charitably. "Our critter ain't going up this dry gulch fer a drink. Charlie's Spring is behind us. He'd have smelled it. Besides, he didn't have to. He knows where water's at. No - he's just a young 'un off prospecting."

I said nothing. Ed rode along glancing from side to side while Shiner teased the cricket in his bit. "He's a black angus cross," Ed announced. "Tufts of hair on the brush," he added in response to my abbreviated snort from the rear. He didn't bother to look back.

"Will I laugh when it turns out to be a red angus cow," I said. "She could have lost her calf and be looking for it."

"You'd hear her beller."

We rode on in continued silence until we came to

a side canyon. Without hesitation Ed took the south fork. No mystery here. My eyes were fixed intently on the ground, firmly resolved to come up with an illuminating observation of my own. The hoof marks were distinct.

"He's lop-horned above the off-ear," Ed proclaimed, "white-faced and stump-tailed."

This was too much. "God damn it, Ed," I blurted with feigned indignation, "you're horse-shitting me. I swapped my swivel-chair for this saddle a long time back. I graduated! Remember?"

"Look up yonder if you don't believe me," Ed said. "He's standing over by that dwarf cedar eyeing us. Better sit quiet for a bit till he gets used to us. We don't want him to take off into the brakes."

There was rarely anything spectacular about a good cowboss, but after riding with one for a time, one began to develop a feeling in his company that can only be described as *awe*. He knew feed conditions in every meadow, canyon and draw and how to fatten a cow on forage where it looked like a jackrabbit would starve. He could ride through a grazing herd and tell which animals had lost weight overnight. He could recognize barren cows from his mental file on their calving records and could name the month, the week and the day the pregnant ones would drop their calves, but he'd be reluctant to forecast the hour. Riding through a sizeable bunch we had brought in from wintering on the flat, Ed Fisher scanned them casually and noted, "Mrs. Gummidge ain't here."

Like Moses, the cowboss could bring forth water

from the rocks, but he didn't need a staff to do it. He could locate every spring, water hole and natural sump in the dark and predict when each would be wet or dry. He was familiar with every swamp, deceptive bog and stretch of quicksand, having pulled some feckless cow or puncher out of them more times than it was worth counting. "Are you addicted to them places?" Ed asked me on one of the several occasions I rode into camp, Gizzard caked to the withers in mud and my boots and chaps similarly embossed.

"It takes a fair hand," Jean volunteered in my defense, "to muscle a smart horse like old Gizzard into one of them doughnut holes."

On cloudless days when even the quakers had quit quaking, the cowboss could smell weather building up - "weather" meaning climate that would make the polar bear-under-glass dividing the casino from the cafe in Elko's Commercial Hotel growl for a parka. In cow country "good weather" was an expression no one ever used. There was heat, cold, wind, dust, rain, sleet and snow - none of which warranted comment. Then there was *weather*, an unconditionally ugly phenomenon. Ed always denied being able to smell a storm brewing. He relied on a variety of empirical data. When the horned toads left signs all pointing south, he'd swear, "They're hell-bent for cover." Or when Emma hung her washing out to dry. Or when his roping arm went stiff. Or when his Stetson became tight on his forehead. Or - or - or. . .

There was sound basis for the cowboss' insights. A widely used sociology text of my generation entitled *Social Thought from Lore to Science* informed us that "science" had replaced ignorance and superstition with knowledge and truth. "Lore" apparently remained locked in the heart of darkness. A cowboss, nevertheless, was a master of lore and it would not indicate back-trailing to the Stone Age if we were to regain respect for it. Science produced the infernal-combustion engine. Lore domesticated the horse. Science cannot risk coping with unquantifiable, uncontrollable variables. Lore can. While science analyzes predicaments, lore extricates one from them without leaving one worse off than he was before. Few scientists will admit that they are guessing. A cowboss will. When the "scientist" shamelessly explains away his erroneous predictions, the cowboss makes no excuses. His hunches are more often right than wrong. He is not rash. He makes sure the kinks are out of the rope before he makes his toss. He'd throw in a hand if the cards didn't seem to mesh with his instinct - even if he'd been the only one at the table with openers. I recollect a scene in which Ed Fisher was mildly reprimanding Henry for having blown his month's wages at the poker table in the old Tonopah Club - and less mildly chastising him for having added his saddle to the pot.

"But, Ed," Henry complained, "whadda y'do when you're holding three queens."

"Eat 'em," Ed said.

So much for lore.

The cowboss was a character mutation - a crossbreed on the psychological level between a man and a horse. Over the years the pair contributed to each others' education and character. The cowboss could interpret the subtle responses of the horse to its surroundings and the horse, in turn, sensed the attitudes of its rider. Where the horse might balk or panic at the scent of danger, his rider could steady him while calmly calculating the risks. Re-assured, the animal was ready to perform feats of equine heroism. Where most horses surrender gumption to greed when exposed to sensual temptation, foundering themselves if a lid has been left off the grain barrel, the cowboss transcended five of the seven deadly sins and by keeping a tight rein on the other two, he transformed them into cardinal virtues. Each entity became mutually dependent upon the other. It was an alliance. But not one established by a scrap of paper. If the bond were broken, both parties suffered permanent injury. And it was never the horse who broke it - unless it had gone mad on loco-weed. This is not intended as a cornerstone for a moral sermon, but it does tell us something about drugs very simply without experimenting on rats and other helpless creatures.

The type of rapport I am attempting to communicate here was experienced by cowhands as well as by cowbosses. The difference was only one of degree. If the premises on which the hypothesis is founded are true, the character of the man will be reflected in the character of the horse. The reverse is also true. But the man is the active and the horse the passive element in the union of the two natures. As Jean Daniels expressed it, "I never knowed a spoiled horse that hadn't been spoilt by some sonovabitch!"

It is not difficult to understand why a good

cowhand was mighty particular about who rode his horse. A good horse can be temporarily "fucked up" by a brute or a fool, but if the exposure has not been lethal or prolonged, his disposition and manners will recover with decent and sensible treatment. A horse is astute at making distinctions and if it has had many different riders it will quickly vary its responses to the man on its back. It is not possible in every instance to predict what the response will be, fury or docility, but it does not act with random caprice. There is always a *reason* for its conduct. "Once a bad horse, always a bad horse," is not true, but as with humans, once serious damage to character has been done, reclamation projects can only have limited success - and then only under extremely exceptional circumstances. Once again, as with so many of the postulations advanced thus far, this subject can only be dealt with adequately through demonstration - the basic objective of *The Leather Throne*. If I mention this often enough I will have to write the book.

Despite outbursts of gluttony, avarice and malicious spite around others of its kind, the cowhorse inspires compassion and admiration. Only an insensitive oaf could fail to be affected by his horse's courage, strength, will-power and stoical capacity to endure indescribable hardships and afflictions. A cowhand who regarded his mount as nothing more than an expendable tool - that is, a cowhand with neither a sense for horses nor horse-sense never made a cowboss - or even a passable cowhand. The cowboss could evoke a horse's latent capabilities for affection, loyalty and intelligence. The attachment that often developed between a man and his horse was not sentimental romanticism, it was transcendental pragmatism. It was fundamental. Neither chance nor privilege made the cowboss the best mounted man in the outfit. It was the splicing of two superior natures. When the horse was displaced by jeeps, choppers, squeeze chutes and cattle trucks, the cowboss did not become obsolete, he became extinct. An essential component of Civilization was lost. Contemporary man - except for a possible relationship with his dog - has fused with the machine and the computer. We are headed for the Black Hole!

iii

It is not true, as Henry Steen bragged while trying to convince his brother Ernie to sign on with the *Fiddleback* instead of the *Lurline*, that "Ed Fisher could rope a buffalo bull out of an open mine shaft it had fell into, sets its busted hump with splints made from sage-brush, flag it off to graze and be back in the saddle before the green-heads could find a landing strip on Shiner's belly."

Proficiency in the skills of his craft and pride of workmanship were, nevertheless, as reflexive in a cowboss as the urge to scratch an itch. With rope, iron, medicine-pouch and his hands and wits, in controlling livestock - and men - he had few peers. He could, however, be occasionally excelled in specific skills by individual members of the crew. This was no disgrace. Every creditable outfit boasted a showcase expert at something - bronc peeling, calf-flanking, steer-roping, ear-marking, honda weaving or working miracles with sourdough. Men were not hired for these accomplishments like many dude ranches signed up talent in the same manner as the Hotel-Casinos of Reno and Las Vegas engage celebrities as tourist attractions. Over-specialization, usually regarded as indicative of a misspent youth, was no asset around a working outfit, but personal distinction in some form of achievement promoted morale. Mediocrities bred pestilence - as everywhere. Exhibitionism, however, was unnecessary and top-hands took pride in retaining their status as versatile amateurs. The rodeo circuit was, at best, an outlet for youngsters overflowing with wild-oat seeds - at worst, a jaundiced career for discontented glory hounds. Home was on the range - not in a trailer parked behind the rodeo-grounds of some commercially ambitious booster-town. The cowboss had survived apprenticeship, run the journeyman's gantlet and outgrown immature compulsions to compete with the jay-birds. It was not important to him to display juvenile prowess at the expense of general competence. "Save the performances for the Fourth," Ed would declare when Henry and Zane would engage in carnival competition while working cattle. "Let's get these critters corraled before the bats come out."

Contrary to formula, it was unnecessary for the cowboss to be able to whip any man in the outfit. A hand who needed whipping didn't belong there in the first place and a cowboss who allowed situations to slip out of control could only have been a relative of the owners. Sore heads eliminated themselves long before anyone had to dehorn them. The cowboss was more adept at keeping the crew out of trouble than emerging from some hooligan fracas bloody, but victorious. To accomplish this he had to keep himself out of trouble. This meant an ability to *hold* his likker - which is not the same as a mythical ability to consume it by the gallon while ineptly simulating an upright posture by sheer effort of a will deprived of its bodily assistance. Jack Chatovich, author or purveyor of verse for all seasons, whose "To a Sego Milk Can" has already been quoted, had the following in his repertoire:

He is not drunk
Who from the floor can rise
To drink once more,
But he is drunk
Who prostate lies
And can neither drink nor rise.

Jack's ditty was, of course, whimsical bravado and had little influence beyond adding the word "prostate" (sic.) to Clarence Genevo's vocabulary. Jean referred to a cowhand heavily under the influence as having "a bad case of staggers." Jean would consume practically a fifth of Cedar Brook every day, but over a ten-year stretch I never saw him "drunk." He would simply become less and less communicative and eventually withdraw to his sod-house. In fact, I never actually *saw* him drink.

"There's hell enough in open country without combing the brush fer it," Ed would caution rambunctious hands on those few occasions we invaded town in a group. Cowboys, however, were not natural brawlers. John Wayne may have used his skull for an anvil on which to smash chairs into kindling and whiskey bottles into ground glass, but screen roughhousing never aroused impulses in anyone to emulate these neanderthal feats. What got a cowhand into trouble was naive honesty, not crude assertiveness that prohibited pulling back one's horns. Cowboys were not playing macho roles. They had uncomplicated convictions which they stood behind with the certainty of one holding a royal flush. They were incredulous if some infidel called their cards. Around cow outfits, good humor and courtesy were valued far more than pugnacity. To be "easy spoke" was a practical virtue. "It didn't pay to be anything else," quoth Teddy Blue Abbott as he pointed them north.

The vulgar belligerence of bar-room culture was a sub-social institution most cowhands chose to avoid. After all, they exiled themselves to dwell in sparse surroundings on sparse fare at sparse wages that kept their stomachs in close proximity to their backbones. Initially, a spirit of adventure may have attracted them to the range. Other sentiments kept them there. That cowboys hankered for a trip to town after weeks of isolation is another figment lent superficial credence by exaggerated accounts of their boisterous visitations on Kansas trail terminals over a century ago and indecently corroborated by Charlie Russell's pictorial clowning. The anecdote of the western bar-tender who told the irate easterner who was complaining about a cowboy invading the premises on horseback, "what do you mean by coming in here on foot anyway?" is a further witty contribution to the popular image. Yet I never knew a puncher who wasn't happier to leave a town than to enter one. If for some innocent reason an outfit's riders began to behave like armed Katzenjammer kids, the cowboss pulled them back from the edge of the rim-rock.

Cowboys were not a troop of equestrian Hell's Angels. They had work to do and it was work that promoted infectious congeniality, ingenuous companionships and general compatability. If nerves became edgy from line-camp fever and absence of the obvious tranquilizer (excessive abstinence constituted a greater threat to the *pax publica* than over-indulgence) a detached, comic sense of the absurd extinguished potentially sanguinary situations. The cowboss, as adept at reading smoke signals as he was at sending them, could turn stampeding tempers by his timely, dessicated humor.

One indelible fall round-up, six of us were marooned at Stone House on the head of Reese River. Twenty years of average annual precipitation funneled itself into twelve days. It would have set a pluvial record for the Toiyabes, but in that remote area nobody bothered to measure it. Rain is no excuse for a lay-off, but cowhands have some human limitations. To round up cattle, it is necessary to find them, and to find and drive them it is necessary to see them. In the thick of a mountain storm at altitudes often above timberlime, visibility approaches zero. So we holed up in an abandoned sheep cabin and waited for the clouds to lift enough to get a horse under them.

For six men, confinement within a 650 cubic foot enclosure with only Zane's dog-eared poker deck and a convenient sack of beans to help pass the time, can erode character. The game, which began as a blessing, soon shed its disguise and by late afternoon of the fourth day almost ended in a spread-misere when Henry was goaded into betting his cherished sorrel mare, Kewpie, against Zane's second-hand, dog-pecker pink cadillac convertible. Nerves were as raw as saddle sores.

At the crucial moment, Ed, who was indulging in one of his frequent breaks from the game, tossed aside the warped, water-stained copy of *Ace High* he had found stuffed in a chink in the wall, yawned and eased from his bunk. "Throw you gear together, boys," he said lazily, "and let's hit the saddle."

It was now dusk and furious spurts of wind-driven rain peppered the old license plates ineffectively patching leaks in the roof. Jean was attempting, unsuccessfully, to smother the smug, satisfied grin of a high-line rider who had just winged the pursuing sheriff leading his bumbling posse. I was conscious of the rattling and shuddering of the buckled stove-pipe and grimly contemplating slinging the cold leather on the wet back of Gizzard who would bust his hinges when you got on him wearing a slicker. It crossed my mind that it was a joke - but with Ed you could never be sure —"

"For christ's aches, Ed," I spluttered, "a pelican wouldn't take off in this downpour."

"We're just shifting camp," Ed said. "It's time we roughed it for a spell."

iv

Fortunately, life is a series of anti-climaxes, disappointing from the viewpoint of literary craftsmanship, but damned welcome to anyone sweating out an actual crisis. We did not shift camp. The crew conducted a successful mutiny against the cowboss. That the mutiny had been deliberately provoked by Ed as a device for deflecting a potentially ugly and uncontrollable situation into a humorous, controllable one was pretty obvious, but the simplicity of the ruse did not detract from the respect we shared for his timing, tact and talent.

The following morning, the storm broke. It continued cold, wet and blustery, but between squalls it was possible to gather stock. Before the round-up was over we were being baked in our skins and basted with dust. Buckarooing subjects man and beast to an endless succession of torments on which Dante's imaginative quill could not have improved. Ed Fisher was a Virgil on horseback. The equanimity of the cowboss was less a model of proper deportment than the attitude of ascetic indifference to terrestrial afflictions characteristic of most older hands and which the younger ones, when schooled by experience, began to appreciate and emulate. Working with a good cowboss revealed life as purpose and accomplishment without forfeiting a subtle, stringent code that took intuitive cognizance of *means*. One learned to accept victories temperately and to lose with dignity. How such a code evolved eludes facile explanation. But it was there, and the cowboss was its embodiment. It was not a role, but it has inspired more "roles" than contemporary society can endure and remain sane. Writers of western fiction have blundered upon peripheral aspects of this ethos and exploited it without comprehension. Literary exploitation, as distinct from literary rendition, is the nemesis of truth. It profits from gross distortion, misrepresentation and outright subversion. Its techniques employ cliches, platitudes and stereotypes - easy detours to circumvent serious thought. The "foreman," if he is not a villain, must announce himself with a slow, misleading drawl or a tough, intimidating bark - Destry or Dunson - Jimmy Stewart or John Wayne. In either case, readers or visual audiences are given to understand that these caricature-heroes mean business! Borden Chase manages to pair both specimens in his pathotypical novel, *Blazing Guns on the Chisholm Trail.* An effective cowboss avoided such absurd extremes that were completely lacking in finesse. As unruffled as a great-horned owl perched in a dead tree, never allowing his voice to rise above a conversational pitch, Ed Fisher was not exactly "easy going." Working with him was exacting - not because he bellowed from the saddle like Dunson bullying his bungling crew into bludgeoning the reluctant herd across Red River, but because he was a perfectionist. Such a designation would not have impressed him and he would probably have denied it. He made allowances for ignorance and errors of judgment, but he took it for granted that one did not make *mistakes.* Once you *knew* your job, there was no excuse for not doing it right. When someone made an error that had no harmful results, his immediate reaction was an amused laughter that was more devastating to the ego than a dressing down from which one could walk away in self-righteous dudgeon. If the error were a serious one, his response was a disquieting silence. Around Ed one was self-intimidated. Dunson, "a bull of a man, a brute of a man," would have botched the crossing with his hot-tempered antics. Only *Jean's Law*, "God protects fools and sonsabitches," would have spared that mounted grizzly from drowning the herd, his horse and himself. Ed operated differently. He performed tasks so flawlessly and inconspicuously that you never realised their difficulty until you attempted them. To elicit from him any overt token of recognition of the usefulness of your existence was worth the sacrifice of a month's wage. It didn't happen very often because his assumption of every member of the outfit's potential excellence made compliments superfluous, if not inane. In the years I rode with him I can only recall it happening twice.

We were scouring the flats for strays that had taken to the brush after we flushed the main bunch out of the mountains in early fall. Quartered at the Home Ranch, we would saddle up before dawn, make our circles and return by sundown. That particular day, I was the last one in. The crew were polishing off a Wiggins version of spotted pup and lick. I plunked down and speared a slab of steak from the platter.

"What did you find?" Ed inquired casually.

"I picked up a cow and calf at Coyote Hole. The calf ain't been branded. It's so damned big it has to find a hollow to kneel down low enough to suck. There was a mighty poor Hip O dry that was dead set on tagging along. I had one helluva time cutting her back or I'd of gotten in hours ago. I run the pair into the barn corral and forked 'em some hay to quiet 'em down."

Jean Daniels had bussed his dishes and was building a smoke. "Take a look at 'em, Jean," Ed said. "Ain't seen a slick-ear on Fiddleback range fer quite a spell."

Jean sauntered out and returned some minutes later. His face was saturnine, his expression wooden. Ed regarded him quizzically. "That there cow you brung in. . ." Jean paused, squinting gravely at his sack of tobacco before tucking it away in his shirt pocket, "bears a powerful resemblance to a two-year old steer."

The braying chorus was instantaneous - as if the crew had been waiting months for the opportunity. "Goddammit," I protested, "that goddam calf clung to that so-called steer like a goddam cockle-burr."

"Well," Ed mused after the hilarity had subsided, "it takes a pretty *goddam* good hand to cut one of John Casey's cows away from her calf."

The other instance was a mite less ambivalent. I had returned from packing salt and was pulling the kyacks off the mules. Ed was hunkered down in the shade of the barn mending a head-stall. "There's about twenty head of Fiddlebacks up in Belcher that I figure hadn't oughta be there," I announced, trying not to make my sense of self-importance appear too obvious.

"How'd you know they was Fiddlebacks," Ed asked.

"Hell," I muttered, suffering a moment of deflation. I had been taken off guard. "They just looked like Fiddlebacks." Hesitant reflection. "I think they had bell-wattles." Further hesitation. "I only saw them from a distance. I was on Bald Ridge with no place to tie the damned mules so I could lope down for a closer look."

"You had a shovel hitched to the pack, didn't you?"

"Yeah. . .?"

Ed silently examined the head-stall while I contemplated what the shovel had to do with it, and the lameness of my phrase, "I *think*. . ." and what had to be Ed's sinister reaction to it.

"Fiddlebacks ain't the only critters in these parts with bell-wattles," Ed eventually remarked, "but we better take a look at 'em. If you'd told me they had a swallow fork on the right, an over-slope and underbit on the left and Fiddleback burned on the right hip, I'd figure you was bluffing. We'll mosey up there in the morning."

When the cows proved to be Fiddlebacks, my feelings were those of a suspected rustler suddenly found innocent and turned loose after having spent the night under a cottonwood with a halter around his neck. Riding back from the basin we took a break in a grassy moraine before stringing the cattle into the narrow canyon. We hadn't exchanged words for some time. Ed offered me his makings. Although I had my own tailor-mades, I gratefully accepted. He fired up, flicked the broken match into the cheerful stream and, with no apparent reference to anything in particular, drawled, "Doc, someday - if you live long enough - you might make a tolerable hand."

V

A peculiar brand of sovereignty, a term that must be kept hobbled, prevailed upon the range. "With studied disregard of authority, a cowboy will do a tremendous amount of work in the line of duty," wrote Dane Coolidge, anthropologist, naturalist, photographer, acute observer and author of some strange gastroscopic western fiction, "but his untamed spirit will not permit him to 'supe' for anybody." As an individual who retained the innards of a cowboy, this also held true of the cowboss. "My idea of a good cowboss," wrote Andy Adams in one of those rare and informed uses of the title, "is a man that doesn't boss any; just hires a first-class outfit of men and then there is no bossing to do." Coolidge's description of the attitudes prevailing around a cow outfit is accurate, but his explanation of them falters. Had independence and contempt for anyone "flashing his star too loud" been inspired only by the cowboy's "untamed spirit" any form of leadership would have been difficult to exercise. To attribute the cowboy temperament to romantic primitivism is erroneous. It is equally erroneous, as is often asserted, to attribute it to the westerner's passion for democracy. The cowboy was neither a Noble Savage nor a Rousseau-ite populist. Squatter, nester, sod-buster and a multitude of caste-oriented epithets are scarcely indicative of egalitarian sentiments and the cowboy relished them all. Conversely, the ironic use of such appelations as head honcho, bug augur, top-screw, buggy boss affirms Coolidge's observation of the cowboy's "studied disregard" for rank, but the animus displayed by use of such appelations was not due to the undisciplined rebelliousness of an untrammeled soul. They were not phrases applied to the cowboss, but to owners, usually absentees, or their administrative representatives. Cowhands recognized need for leadership. What they despised was unmerited authority, the preponderent conjunction of incompetence with power. An astute proprietor would have arrived at Andy Adams' conclusion on his own and by-passed hierarchical managerial flunkies (or "foremen") and placed total confidence in the judgment of a cowboss who had the respect and good-will of the crew. Owners of this type were scarce because in most cases ownership was either divided or vested in "Land and Cattle Companies" that were abstract creations of financial investment enterprises and not flesh-and-blood "cowmen." As for the remaining cases of individual ownership, wisdom has never been a quality in adequate supply anywhere.

Under ideal conditions, the job of cowboss was *assumed* reluctantly by some venerable top-hand with knowledge, skill, prudence and a modest amount of charysma who could be expected to "prove up" on the task. The individual naturally singled out for the role of cowboss inevitably became the outfit's honored and esteemed scapegoat - the man condemned to argue with skunks, badgers, mules and the cook. Anyone eager for the distinction involuntarily disqualified himself. Thus, except on guest ranches where dude-wrangling corrupted the entire operation, envy, professional jealousy, back-biting and status rivalry were non-existent - along with reverence, blind or feigned.

Such was life on the Fiddleback. And in case one of my premises has become obscure, I am contending that the nature of the life on the old time spreads tended to produce harmony and compatability. Incompetence, undependability, pettiness and malice were swamped out by a combination of the laws of natural selection and human gravitation. It was a self-purifying process. My popularity with academic colleagues was not enhanced when I would tactlessly tell them that if a cowhand was as inept at his work as they were at theirs he would be, if lucky, out of a job - otherwise dead! Institutionalized society mothers the weak or, *worse,* has changed the definition of "strength."

It is not my intention to present the Fiddleback as a utopia or to maintain that cowbosses were saints-on-horseback. Bob Lee may help keep us from losing a stirrup. Bob Lee occasionally punched cows for the Fiddleback. He was no vagabond. He was neither shiftless nor irresponsible. He was a nomad. The world for which his character and abilities were suited dissolved around him. He was a top-hand who survived beyond his era by a slim margin. He'd worked all over the west for some of the great outfits and he'd known some noteworthy cowbosses. Next best to working for them, he liked to talk about them. Tapes had not come into fashion when we used to "h'ist a few" together, but if I'd had one he wouldn't have talked into it and would have regarded me as some sort of freak for packing it around. Dane Coolidge had similar trouble with his camera. Anyway, one night we got to chewing the cud - and the subject was "cowbosses-I-have-knowed."

"Charlie Wallace wasn't the worst cowboss I ever rid for," Bob announced with excessive gusto. "Charlie Demmick was. So damned persnickety - and *clean*." The inflection on the italicised adjective was not meant to excite my veneration. "Sat his horse perked up like a ground squirrel on sentry duty. Every night before bedding down he'd sneak off and wash at whatever spring or water-hole was available. Carried a little tin mirror to shave with. Smart enough not to pack a glass one. Always shining it on his sleeve. There'd be times you'd spot a flash bouncing off some hog-back and you'd know he was up there preening. He kept a pin-striped mustache trimmed like a french gigolo. Don't know why. He wasn't interested in women - or anybody for that matter. Horses and cows were all that concerned him besides hisself. Coyotes, maybe. He had a soft spot for them shifty varmints. Never let a hand take a shot at one. Claimed they was smarter, tougher and more self-sufficient than people. He liked to hear their yelping chorus before daybreak. They were his alarm clock - and he was ours."

"Didn't he ever worry about coyotes getting at his calves?"

"I asked him that once, and you know what he said?"

"I only read a person's mind when he's in the room."

"He said, 'if I raise a cow that can't protect her calf from a coyote, I get rid of that cow!' Christ, but he was an arrogant sonovabitch." Bob laughed. It was really more of a guffaw. "He was right though, by god! That's a cowman for you. Not one of these sniveling cow farmers that are taking over the country and calling themselves ranchers." Charlie Demmick's Boswell fixed a grip on the neck of the bottle like he was steadying a rooster's head for the impending blow of the axe and continued his fiery eulogy. "The worst thing about Demmick was that goddamn sheepskin." The indignant puncher downed his drink and hammered the glass on the bar for increased emphasis. "Yes. He'd have this stinking sheepskin tied to the seat of his saddle with rawhide." He paused. "Come to think of it, that was why he'd have to douse himself so often." While reflecting on this illuminating discovery, Bob Lee refilled his glass. "Another thing about him that would make you as mad as a riled hornet," he resumed, "whenever he'd tell you where to ride - which was pretty damned condescending of him because ninety-nine percent of the time he'd expect you to conjure the word from your medicine pouch or toss a pointed stick into the wind and see which way it come down - anyhows, he'd turn away from you as if you had breath like a hound that had been eatin' on buzzard-bait. You couldn't hear what he'd be muttering. If you guessed what you was supposed to do and guessed wrong, he'd read the scriptures all over your hide - the hell's fire and damnation parts. I hated to ride with the bastard. He was a rough 'un to keep up with."

Though acting disgruntled, Bob fondled his freshly emptied glass affectionately. "That on'ry, alkalied cuss packed a full spread of horns with more rings than you'd find on a rich madam. Talked like one of them Bengal Lancer chaps. I think he come from Canada someplace - north of Calgary. Used to tell us we all rode as if our spinal columns had been removed. Sarcastic little shit, he was. But he sure knew his cows. He'd never throw his saddle on the ground. In camp, if there weren't a freshly scrubbed rock or a waxed and polished log to sit on, he'd stand up to eat." Bob's sentences were coming forth in isolated fragments until with a sudden flourish he exclaimed, "By god, let's drink to them poor benighted sinners inhabiting the forty sections of hell he's now riding. When I check in, I hope they assign me to a different part of the spread. But I wouldn't want to meet up with Charlie Wallace either. Now take Charlie Wallace... ."

We will spare readers, if at this point there are any still with us, the equally laudatory and lugubrious testimonial to the memory of Charlie Wallace for a more favorable occasion. Besides, his profile is unnecessary. If Demmick was the worst cowboss Bob Lee could dredge from his past, the point is made. On the way back to the ranch, I asked him who he considered the *best* man he had ever ridden for. He was non-committal. I had insisted upon leaving the dregs of the bottle at Carver's, thus producing a mildly sulky mood. Moreover, a cowhand is more adept at ridicule than he is at bestowing praise. I've never heard one lionize or enshrine anybody - including Teddy Roosevelt.

"Can't really say," Bob eventually grumbled. "They were all pretty fair hands, I guess. Course, whenever I come up against a real cotton-mouth I'd just quit. I've ridden for some with enough sand and savvy to dam the Canyon." His spirits began to revive as he talked. "That was a fool notion of yours to leave that bottle back there. Ed comes pretty close. I figure that's what you want to hear. He overdoes that easy-spoke routine. He ought to kick the shit out of Zane. But, hell! There ain't no *best*. I can't think of nobody that'd make Ed take second money."

Owners, unless they were courting bankruptcy, did well to respect the tender loyalties of such punchers as Bob Lee. They did not appoint a cowboss as a reward for subservience, or as a sinecure for one of their wives' indignant relatives, or as a titular concession to a leaking ego. Multiple vice-presidencies might adorn the rosters of corporate institutions whose urbanized structures, from the perspective of the saddle, retained stability only because of the social order's liason with facade and deceit. In cow country rank ranked with the four-card flush. Cowhands shared a sharp nose for the first whiffs of despotism and were alert to the insidious psychological processes by which fraudulent distinctions, conferred upon non-entities, fan the coals of self-importance into the flame of petty tyranny. They may never have read the *Constitution*, but they empathized with its intent and had no use for law-wranglers who connived in its abuse. Every cowhand I knew would have welcomed an opportunity to hang every holder of public office and sign a new *Declaration of Independence*. They shied from every symbol of cant and humbug however gaudily decked out. Even sober words like "wagon boss" and "range boss" were abandoned when there was no longer a wagon in operation and the range had become fragmented into fenced pastures. The Fiddleback, in addition to several "fields," had a Small Pasture and a Big Pasture. The Small Pasture consisted of five thousand acres of mixed grass, swamp and buckbrush. Dudes who occasionally encroached upon our privacy were allowed to play cowboy in it. The cows couldn't go anywhere and if the dudes failed to show before dark they could easily be found. As long as there were cows left with sufficient freedom from enclosure and mechanical innovations to be able to challenge the ingenuity of their human oppressors, there was need for a cowboss.

"Foreman" was a title grudgingly acknowledged, but never accepted as a substitute for "cowboss." An impugnable witness in support of this heretical contention is the unblemished chronicler of the day of the cattleman, Andy Adams. In a tale, "Alkaline Dust Ain't Snow," the terms "cowboss" and "foreman" are both used, but not interchangeably. The former is used in an approved manner, the latter in a derogatory sense. "Don't you know, sir, that I'm in authority here?" raps the foreman.

"Well, if you are, no one seems to respect your authority, as, you're pleased to call it, and I don't know of any reason why I should," the affronted cowhand replies.

The foreman was an alien intruder. His tradition was not of the saddle. He was not a descendent of the trail or wagon boss, but a product of the transition from the nomadic culture to settled, institutionalized ranching. The cowboss and the foreman performed in separate spheres. The latter became responsible for all operations exclusive of handling cattle and was regarded by the cowhands as the whipping-boy for a glorified sod-buster. As late as 1965 I encountered buckaroos who declined to eat or bunk with the ranch hands - at least until the hay-crew had departed and farming activities had shut down for the season. It was an affectation sustained by their jaded identification with the exclusivist tradition of the past. To borrow from Jean Daniel's private lexicon, a foreman was "a feller who wintered near the stack, bedded in clean straw and had allowed himself to be broke to the point that any man, woman or child could ride him right into the barn." Today this is true of the whole crew.

"Ramrod," is a flinty term popularized by low-grade fiction. After castigating three respectable references for neglecting to include "cowboss" in their collections, it may seem wanton to commend them for omitting "ramrod." But it is a bastard expression. Buckaroos were not particularly offended by it because outside of the commercial "oater" they were seldom confronted by it. R.J. Symons conferred sham respectability on "ramrod" by admitting the imposter to his glossary appended to *Where the Wagon Led.* The synthetic image of an insensible length of steel pounding a powder-charge into the barrel of an unreliable muzzle-loader is a symbol grossly inexpressive of the relationship between a cowboss and his salty crew. The image, however, was probably only meant to indicate that the outfit wouldn't "fire" without him.

Apart from philological interest the place of "ramrod" in the vocabulary of the cattle world is inconsequential. Its functional ambiguity caused it to atrophy. As a word descriptive of the character of the cowboss it was incongruous, and as slang for "foreman" it endowed the latter with more prestige and importance than cowhands were inclined to grant him. If they used the term at all, it was always with a touch of irony. Only script writers took the term seriously. Dunson!

"That feller ramrodded hisself up his own ass," was Holly Richardson's bizarre comment after he had finished reading Chase's gusty yarn.

What is less inconsequential is that outfits in which the cowboss became subordinated to the foreman, or in which their functions were indecently fused, were in the process of being transformed into branches of agro-industry and the unique contributions of the cattle frontier to the American heritage were over. The urban-industrial-commercial predilections of writers of western fiction prevented them from differentiating between a cowboss and a foreman. Their interest in the West in general and cowboys in particular was not even a genuine case of nostalgia. They were intent upon selling books so they could live high on the hog that American capitalism was fattening beyond all conceivable dreams. This meant exploiting the melodramatic possibilities of the men and the setting without bothering to understand either. Recognition of the fact that the cowboss remained a cowboy and differed from his crew only to the extent that the nucleus differs from the cell was not only unimportant, it was detrimental to a plot formula that was being dictated by values alien to the line-camp. But the cowboss did remain a cowboy with the cowboy's outlook.

Unlike the rancher compelled to regard cows as units of salable beef-on-the-hoof, the cowboss looked upon them with the eye of the artist. Although the cowboss was usually asked to pronounce on the readiness of cattle for the market, that was not the goal for which he had striven. His satisfaction came from being able to ride through a herd which, under his vigilant care, exhibited uniform fitness - grace - perfection. Con Price tells the story of two city men over-awed by the scenic grandeur of the grazing lands through which they were being escorted. One of them, in a compulsive, euphoric outburst, exclaimed, "Isn't that the most beautiful sight you ever saw?"

"The purtiest thing I ever saw," the taciturn cowboss accompanying them replied, "was a fat, four year old steer."

I knew one tough cowboss who would bawl every time the beef-cut was shipped. Some ranchers felt the same way. They were ambivalent fellows who would have preferred to remain cowboys than to succumb to the mandatory values of a business civilization. But, as Jean Daniels expressed it *in requiem,* "they got theirselves tangled in a clothesline."

vi

The cowboss has not become a universal folk hero, but he was the stuff from which folk heroes should be made. Unfortunately the bards "done him wrong." In a recent footnote added to that endless squabble between custodians of the historical West and the promoters of the legendary West, "The West That Wasn't," C.L. Sonnichsen defends bigamy. "What we find hard to admit," he contends, "is that we hold dual citizenship and are quite comfortable in our two wests - that we want and need each of them; that our national well-being depends to some extent on maintaining free access to both, the unreal as well as the real one. If we did not have a phony West to fall back on, we would be in a bad way. . . The West that Wasn't remains so much a part of American consciousness that no infusion of realism can take it away. We can't and won't give it up because we need it."

There are too many frayed strands on this scratchy cinch to carry Sonnichsen's argument through a crow-hop. Sane individuals must disclaim membership in that schizoid brotherhood unaccountably referred to as "*we*." Who are these bicephalous somnambulists compacently comfortable in contradictory Wests? What is the "need" this amorphous "*we*" has for both - and what, precisely, is the "bad way" in which that same "*we*" would find themselves without the phony West to fall back on? How does our "national well-being" depend upon our freedom to drug ourselves with nonsense to the degree that the nation's president could boast without blushing that he would "get out of Viet Nam, guns blazing, like a cowboy backing out of a saloon."?

If we have a national problem, it is one we share with much of mankind - self-deception. We have one West too many. The phony one. Myth does not have to be phony. Valid myth is a metaphorical dramatization of insights derived from reality. *The Emperor's New Clothes* portrays a universal aspect of human experience. *Gunslinger Rides Again* does not. Myth distills meaning from history at the point where academic historians unsaddle. A civilized society should view with suspicion both a vulgarized mythology *and* the dehumanized abstractions of "social" and "behavioral sciences." When we brutalize our historical legacies in the name of art, science or business we betray the present and future. The past is locked in its unquiet grave. A legion of hucksters have been debauching a susceptible, critically impoverished public for so long that we are in danger of losing our moral inheritance altogether. Representations of the cowboy have vilified a personality whose genuine stature surpasses in nobility the mock heroics of theatrical buffoons released from the chutes by entrepreneurs of the entertainment industry. To redeem this hostage to the mass mind requires a campaign practically no one believes can be won. It is combat in the ethical sector of the crusade against the rampant pollution of civilized life by unremitting and unregenerate commercialism. The task brings to mind the cowboss who came upon a bog-rider's stetson adrift on the mud wallow. With a toss of his rope he began to retrieve it when he heard a half-suffocated voice, "Never mind the hat, just get your loop fixed to pull me and my horse out of here."

Grossness and depraved taste seem here to stay. Nevertheless, behind the burlesque cowboy superstar, there was a nimble-witted Spartan whose ethical stability matched his physical stamina. His model was the cowboss - an individual who conducted himself according to independent, time-enduring standards instead of allowing himself to become a fixture in a social order hypnotized by the gospel of expediency. Most contemporary intellectuals are confused and contaminated by some variant of the heresy according to which personal responsibility for sin is disavowed. These stunted materialists assume man to be a creature programmed by his genetic "code," his bowel training, his environment or some unfathomable combination of external forces beyond his control. There is no unfenced range for the mind and the will as autonomous creative agents. Sartre attempted to invert these deterministic formulas for despair, but seems to have generated only a passing intellectual fad.

It is folly to attempt to recover your tobacco when it has blown away in a dust-storm. The tidal wave of population and the excremental profusion of industrial technology have reduced the individual to a midge. But the cowboss was no midge. He was nature's existentialist. When Ed Fisher chose for himself, he chose for the outfit. Despite the spacial magnitude of the world within which Ed functioned, it was still a microcosm replete with tangible objectives that could be achieved with that surplus yardage of guts and the brains to know when to put them into action. It would be a mistake, however, to infer that the cowboss' virtues were occupational, applicable only to the times and conditions from which they derived. On the contrary, his virtues were those that have characterized all the inconspicuously great men throughout recorded history. They were the virtues displayed by Mr. Roberts when he threw Captain Morton's potted palms overboard, demonstrating one clear exception to Saul Bellow's suspicion that literature in democratic society lost the capacity to conceive of the heroic. Mr. Roberts would have made a fine cowboss and a good cowboss would also have thrown those symbolically accursed potted palms overboard. The only difference is that the cowboss, unhampered by naval canons and punctilio, would have thrown them over sooner and Captain Morton along with them.

"One time I was riding circle below the South Rim," Ed Fisher recollected gravely. "I got to watching this cat-eyed squaw beating a dead mule. She was helping out her willer stick with some mighty powerful tongue medicine." It was considerable before sunup and cold enough to freeze whatever snake-head whisky was left in your bladder from the night previous. If there's no wind, cold weather is no worse than most other kinds. But we could hear that mixed up wailing, whining and whistling outside - the sort of zephyr that won't lie down and be quiet long enough to roll a smoke. We were hugging the pot. Any excuse to put off saddling up. There was a prolonged, guilty silence, mostly due to our general awareness that Ed knew we were dragging our tails.

"What happened," Henry eventually asked when it was evident that Ed didn't intend to continue until somebody was curious and rash enough to stick his head out of his hole.

"It got up." Ed said.

Readers can cut Ed's fable any direction they please, but as we hunched our way toward the corral, Jean muttered as much to himself as to the rest of us, "After they made Ed, they threw away the mold."

Covering the Dog...

. . . is an expression borrowed from range lingo to top off what otherwise would have been afflicted with the raw label, "appendix." In spite of everything I have written attesting to their gumption, incredulity and aversion to humbug, even cowhands are not immune to the hypnotic power of the correct label. Fine feathers may not make fine birds, but there was always the fact to be considered that a navvy was a navvy and wouldn't do for riding the river. In matters of attire, the sorry condition of one's harness did not diminish one's stature because it was taken as a badge differentiating the legitimate cowhand from a spraddled-out dude. As a mark of distinction, spruce clothing was insignficant compared to such approved tags as Justin, Nocona, John B, Levi Strauss and so forth. This was also true of saddles. Labels were called "brands" and like brands, once established, they stuck! A cowhand's pig-headed loyalties were not deterred by his shrewd reason, they just rambled over it like cows ignoring loose wire. Instead of stopping to tighten fence, we'll go on —

At the end of fall round-up, Ed Fisher used to say, "Well, I guess that about covers the dog." The derivation of the cryptic expression is enshrouded in mystery. Jean Daniels, who would swallow a dry toad before he'd lie to himself, maintained that it was lifted from the argot of the sheep-camp.

"'Steb' Vasquez would use them words all the time - whether he was calling a feller's poker hand or locking horns with some hombre he'd figured had run off with his hog. No self-respecting cowhand would threaten to cover your dog. He'd say, 'I'm gonna hang up your hide'."

"Ed Fisher says it," Henry interjected slyly, gloating at the thought that he'd slicked Jean into the squeeze-pen.

"Nobody's perfect," Jean replied flatly, swallowing another terrestrial amphibian as if it had been a raw egg in a glass of soured milk.

"Okay," I put in while Henry was reflecting that before running Jean into the chute, he should have shut the gate at the other end, "suppose it is a sheepherder's phrase, it still doesn't make sense."

Jean regarded me as though I belonged in the

nursery pasture along with the rusties. "Look at it this way," he explained. "The most valuable asset of a sheepherder is his dog. When he says he's covered his dog, he's telling you he buried it. It's like a cowhand hollerin' calf rope. He's run afoul of the Devil on a one-way ledge. He ain't got enough wind left to drag his tail over fine dust. He's finished."

"Maybe," I conceded with mock sincerity. "But it isn't that sinister when Ed says it. He's simply indicating that we've completed a job."

"I ain't saying that Ed thinks we're about to join a funeral procession when he says it," Jean continued. "You asked me where I thought the saying come from and I'm telling you how 'Steb Vasquez meant it. I ain't responsible for what folks does to perfectly good language and I give up a long time ago expecting 'em to make sense. When 'Steb' writes his name out, he spells it E-s-t-e-b-a-n and pronounces it Estevan, and then he writes V-a-s-q-u-e-z and pronounces it Basketh. Take you f'rinstance. Until I couldn't stand it no more and instructed you different, you kept a-sayin' 'ornery' when it's 'on'ry'."

"Everybody says 'ornery'," Henry said. "Zane says 'ornery'."

"Zane ain't everybody - although he's more like everybody than anybody," Jean corrected, "and even if they did, all it'd prove is that there's times everybody can be wrong. But things ain't that bad. The worst a hand can hold with is that most people are wrong most of the time."

"That'd be worse!" Henry erupted with sprightly enthusiasm. Two rash skirmishes had not convinced him to abandon the field. "If everybody was wrong at the same time, they might all be right at other times. But if its like you say, that most of the people are wrong most of the time, that ain't so good. Because we got democracy and that means most people run the show - and that means they run it *all* the time. So if they're wrong most of the time that'd mean we was running a pretty seedy outfit."

I wanted to shake out my own loop on this one, but Jean was ahead of me and still had his eye on the same critter that was dodging in and out of our discussion. "That could be," he agreed, brushing Henry to one side. "Most people got so many holes in their heads you couldn't pour instant brains into one fast enough to keep it from sifting out the others. But you don't hear Emma, or Ed, or Harry, or even Wiggins saying 'ornery.' On'ry ain't a short-cut for 'ordinary' like Doc was arguin' from a book he'd read it in someplace."

"*Webster's New World Dictionary,*" I muttered feebly.

"It's an entire different word," Jean went on. "My old man, he used it regular. Only a lot of the time he'd say 'on'rous.' According to him most everyone who come by our place was 'an on'rous sonovabitch.' I'd get to thinking he was probably more on'rous than any of 'em. But I guess that's what comes of always being right when most everyone else is sufferin' from hollow-horn."

Jean reached out and poked the coals with a stick as if probing for something among the cinders. "The old man never went around looking for dogs to kick.

I'll say that for him." Jean continued to ruminate on the edges of his obscure past. "Fact is, it was the other way 'round. He was always stopping other folk from doing the kicking. He busted up a self-appointed hemp-committee once. They was about to string up a local sheepherder. The old man sure as hell hated sheep crowding the ranges - not for what they et - sheep are browsers more'n grazers and don't argue with cows much over the delicacies. It was the solid mass of 'em that would put the hump in his back - and how they trompled and pissed every place until the valleys was a stinking mat of useless fodder. He was agin' working off his froth by taking it out on the chili-eaters that herded them though. This poor greaser they'd slipped the halter on hadn't done no more than take a shot at the sneakin' varmints who'd been killing his dogs. The old man didn't cotton to that either. He didn't hold with any kind of bush-whacking - man nor beast. We were out hunting dogs once - that's ground-squirrels I'm referrin' to, not sheep dogs. He'd been standing with his rifle tucked loose and lazy into his shoulder without drawing a bead for what seemed to me a long enough spell to freeze a barrel of hard cider at thirty above. So I up and shot it myself. He cussed me thoroughly. 'Why didn't you shoot?' I grumbled. I was mad as a diamond-back with someone standing on its rattles. 'I give you plenty of time. Hell, I thought you didn't see it.' 'I was giving it a chance to get a running start,' he said. The old man was downright or'ry in his way. But there weren't nothing ordinary about him. No whit!"

"Them mules is powerful quiet," Henry said, looking out over the moon-drenched meadow from our compact camp on the outer fringe of a copse of willows. "Maybe I better take a look at 'em."

"You'd hear 'em if they was fussed," Jean said, commencing to build himself a smoke. "You'd be powerful quiet yourself if you was shod with iron boots and made to pack four fifty-pound salt blocks to the tops of them bare ridges over rock that was hot enough to curl bacon. They're relaxin' and peaceful fer once. Let 'em alone."

It was mid-July and the three of us, at Ed's suggestion, had taken advantage of the lull between the first and second cuttings to make the circuit of the Toiyabe salting grounds. We had horses and three mules. Henry and I were scattering the blocks and every third day one mule got a day off, a privilege denied their two-legged oppressors. Jean was along as Ed's viceroy checking out the cows on summer range. Packing salt was a slow job, but Jean was always back to camp early to do the cooking and the expedition would have to be classified as a leisurely outing. Work with a moderately sized range outfit defies standard descriptive powers. There is an elusive human need that derives peculiar gratification from concentrating on a single, arduous task that combines utility with pleasure - or, put another way, the pleasure itself is derived from productive physical exertion that is not so strenuous as to anaesthetize the senses, and not of such routine monotony as to deaden the mind. I understand why cowhands seldom ride a horse for recreation and look askance at the frivolous equestrian enthusiasm of dudes. I have come to feel (not "think") that way myself. For one thing, meaningless pleasures do not "re-create." This attitude was neither an occupational affectation nor the reaction of a person who had to get away from his *job* and anything associated with it. To the cowhand, his work wasn't something that it was necessary to escape from. He may have enjoyed occasional bouts with the town - or embarked on some extended, capricious adventure. But he did not take *vacations*. He needed a vacation like he needed to join a union, or to shoot his horse so he would not have to ride it all the way back to the ranch from the line-camp.

The sense of fulfillment and satisfaction that came from sharing that angst-free life with the intrepid jesters who haunt these pages has never been experienced since. No doubt that is why I am compelled to write about it. The frantic pleasure lusts and the rage to live of so many of my urban acquaintances, and the revolting sums they manage to squander for over-priced equipment wherewith to despoil and devastate the environment - especially the serene majesty of what once could be called wilderness, never ceases to offend my puritan spirit that venerates beauty and abhors waste. This is not a digression. I am revealing thoughts evoked by the cinnabar glow of our diminutive fire, the only purpose of which was to provide a winsome focus for companionship and to keep the pot warm - because the night, an unguent after the fierce heat of the day, was bright enough, as Jean remarked, "to read the fine print in a prayer book." By four in the morning we would be up frying an aromatic breakfast. Anyone who has not savored the silent magnitude of pre-dawn, not from a metal camper parked on a turn-out within convenient sight of a "rest-room," but as the ever-changing overture to a working day in a remote line-camp, has not lived for any more exalted purpose than to be able to vote for Reagan.

Some one, at this point, is certain to play the game that Eric Berne could have called, "if you don't like it here, whey don't you go to Russia?" I did not voluntarily abandon that life. It was embezzled from me - as it was from Ed, Jean, Henry, Holly, Zane and a retinue of ambulatory acolytes who used to make seasonal appearances at the Fiddleback. It was eroded by the country's voracious craving for a bloated GNP and the pursuit of the most gargantuan euphemism of all, *Progress.* After the decay of the Fiddleback, I scouted a few other outfits. They were all tainted cow factories. I made adjustments. One could say that I copped out. But I didn't commit that most venal sin present society extolls as a virtue, "If you can't beat 'em, join 'em." When Jean Daniels reached the end of a life that fate had reduced to a meaningless rasp, he reached for a shotgun rather than succumb to the barbiturates and butcheries of an over-crowded hospital. Few of us have that sort of guts. Anyone who tells me that suicide is the coward's way out makes me want to put on war-paint and uproot the tomahawk. But on that limpid night, camped at Rogers' Meadow, Jean was still with us and breaking in on my troubled reflections.

"It just don't make sense to argue that on'ry has

anything to do with "ordinary," he was still insisting, like old Rex-dog worrying a stubborn bone. "Reminds me of one time Doc here was talking sense and cut Zane down to size for saying that the exception proves the rule."

"They was arguin' about how them cows could of got into the hay corral without someone leaving the gate open," Henry chuckled. "I remember. Zane had fed that morning and if the gate was left open it had to have been him that done it. So first Zane says the cows must of knocked it down. Then Ed says that no cow could bust down *that* gate. Then Zane comes up with that exception proves the rule shit. That was about the time Doc took off on his spiel. It was pretty funny."

Jean emitted one of his snorting laughs. "Doc was plumb right fer once."

"I'm right almost all the time," I grunted. "You half-literate bastards just hate to admit it."

"I ain't so sure about that," Jean said, "but sometimes you make sense - especially if it ain't too important. If there's an exception, it stands to reason there ain't no rule. How can an exception prove a rule? But people sez it all the time. You might just as well say the best way to cook a steak is to eat it raw. I forget how you explained how come people who are supposed to have some intelligence make such foolish statements without never bothering to think. But they sure as hell do."

"Your example isn't as good as your point, Jean," I answered. "Actually 'the best way to cook a steak is to eat it raw' makes a kind of sense regardless of whether anyone agrees with you or not. It's the sort of ironic remark *you* in particular make frequently. What you could be implying is that a good steak is better eaten raw than burning hell out of it. It's a different type of statement than the one I objected to. The contradiction in 'the exception proves the rule' is due to a misconception of the meaning of the word 'prove' in that particular context. When that phrase was minted, 'prove' was a synonym for 'test.' Properly interpreted it meant that the validity of an asserted rule is tested by exceptions. The phrase means exactly the reverse of what Zane thought he was saying. The same could hold true for 'covering the dog.' If 'covering' means burying and it is a sheepherders dog, then the words don't indicate the successful completion of a task, but a ruinous disaster."

"I'm about to cover this dog," Jean said. "You've near put me to sleep. If you was as good a roper as you are at partin' out words and locoed notions, you'd be a top hand."

"Roping is defunct," I retaliated. "In ten years all you cowhands with obsolete skills will be on the drift or on the county. I'll still be on civilization's pay-roll. No matter if the world goes to hell, brains will always be needed. Especially when it goes to hell!"

"Brains may be needed," Jean quipped, "but nobody'll want 'em." He heaved himself to his feet. "All your words ain't gonna do you no good a-tall - unless you can rest easy just playing games with 'em. But you got to keep talking turkey to fellers like Henry here who don't want to do nothin' but ride the shows."

"What's wrong with wanting to ride the shows?"

Henry demanded beligerently. "Casey Tibbs, he. . ."

"Nothin' - if it don't go no further than wantin'," Jean said. "What's more, you ain't Casey Tibbs. You're a cowboy. Or what we've got to use for one."

"I can at least make my beans on the circuit," Henry persisted. "Doc's right. Cowboyin's played out. What happens to us and the Fiddleback when old Emma gets the deed to her claim on bone hill?"

"You'll all be a-wonderin' who lifted your hair." Jean shook his head in disgust. "I won't be around nohow. Right now I'm hittin' the blanket." He headed for his spot in the brush.

ii

Jean's disquisition raises questions I have no intention of burdening readers with as we grind up these switchbacks. Instead, I'm going to rustle Henry's defence of the confusing twists in his unresolved mustang yarn. He had explanations for all the incongruities stored in his mental attic, but was sufficiently merciful to spare his audience the tedium of listening to him lay them out. Henry appealed for equitable trust, but did not really give a damn if he got it or not. *He* knew what he was talking about and if the gallery chose to feign ignorance and demonstrate true malice by pouncing on him at every favorable opportunity that was their privilege. "Fuck you shitheads," was the brash core of his creed and character and one had to admire his undaunted nerve. I lost track of him before he was out of his twenties and would feel comforted to know that he never lost his independent spirit under the bludgeoning of a sordid social order. His attitude was not that of crude, juvenile arrogance. He did not have contempt for us. His was the pity that a charitable believer has for the infidel hopelessly deprived of faith in the promise of salvation. Henry had fortitude, determination, humor, optimism, guts and gumption. His folly was that his ambitions and virtues were oriented to a world in dissolution. The last time I saw him, he was pumping Maverick Gas at a superstation in Bishop. There the atrophied cowboy was swinging a hose instead of his rope and wiping windshields for well-marbleized unisex *turistas* while they bee-lined for the rest-rooms in their bermuda shorts, aloha shirts and *huaraches.* He'd brought his fiddle to the party, but no one asked him to play.

Here I am explaining Henry instead of resting content with displaying him in action and allowing readers to fit him into their own frames. Ed Fisher's verdict on me goes down like a fried egg dropped in sand. I would be chagrined to acknowledge myself a victim of the "intellectual" plague of our age - the sadistic determination to explain everything to everyone, eradicating all mystery and destroying the joys of individual discovery in the name of science and "democracy" while leaving life a bigger muddle than it has been at any time in the past.

I lack Henry's audacity. Although he frequently told us what we could go and do to ourselves (without *explaining* how it was to be done), you may recall that he made allowances for our skeptical doubts about the career and prowess of Cerulean Copulator and deigned to offer casual clues to adumbrate the action and to recommend that we suspend our hasty judgments until he had mustered all his data into a meaningful pattern. But he'd be damned if he'd wallow in the slime of *mea culpa.*Readers are entitled to a reasonable amount of explanation and writers have some justification for making reasonable demands upon readers. Notice that I have carefully avoided alluding to "rights" possessed by either party. We should be less concerned with "rights" and more concerned with "reciprocal obligations." This way there might be a chance of restoring a moral social order. It would place responsibility back where it belongs - on individuals rather than on government and the law. The concept of "rights," a well-intentioned device to protect individuals from abuses of *power*, was an arrow that missed its mark. It proved to be an insidious innovation that warped human relationships in a mechanistic society. Life on the Fiddleback was not simplistic primitivism. Everyone was *civilized* in the ethical (fundamental) sense of the term. No one needed his "rights" protected from anyone else. A fraternal understanding existed among all the members of this small colony - a condition I found lacking or reduced to sterile protocol in academic instutions, large or small. This reference to the teaching profession is introduced only to explain why I explain. After all, I was trained as an educator before I acquired much experience as a cowhand. I regret that it was not the other way around. The best thing that ever happened to me was getting fired from the faculty of the University of Nevada. The procedure is not called "firing" or even "dismissal." One's "contract" is simply "not renewed," in my case for "budgetary reasons." In those days of the pogroms of Joe McCarthy and Harold Velde the university administration deliberately blurred the differences between enlightened conservatism and communism. Any manifestation of independence of mind was judged subversive. Henry Steen's attitude was mentally and morally healthy. With minor lapses into infantilism, so was that of the entire crew. No one wanted to purge anyone - even Wiggins. An impressive aspect of the Fiddleback outfit was the ability of the group to retain a high regard for individual character and initiative while demonstrating a spontaneous community of values and purpose in practice. This is treacherous terrain. I'm not spouting hokum about "togetherness" (there wasn't any) or "duty to one's country" (there wasn't any). But there was something else. There were no barriers. Nothing was contrived. Loyalty to the Fiddleback was loyalty to "an outfit" and the outfit was a symbol of a composite way of life that each understood and cherished. I'm not talking about "democracy" either, or "communism," those meaningless shibboleths evoked by scoundrels and fools to sanction policies and practices that by any other standards would be considered barbaric lunacy. That wages were equal, that Emma Rogers "owned" the Fiddleback, that Ed Fisher made most of the decisions were incidental and, as far as they affected the sense of unity, inconsequential. Proceeds from cattle sales all flowed to Emma - as did the bills. There were too many years in which the latter outran the former, but no matter. In the long run all income sustained the Fiddleback. There were no remittances to indolent nephews, no doles, no investing of surplus funds for personal gain, no hording. Emma kept all money in a safe on the premises and if she had disclosed the combination to anyone it was a secret that never aroused any curiosity. She hated banks - with reason! Whatever the Fiddleback produced in excess of what it consumed (profit) was filched from it by the industrial and distributing institutions of which it was a victim, but there was one breed of predator Emma believed that she was not compelled to feed - the Banks. That these pantophagous leviathans gouged her indirectly through the prices she had to pay for equipment was a fact she shut from her mind. "If you can't see it, don't let it bother you," she would huff.

"That doesn't make sense, Emma," I would argue helplessly. "When you can't see the thief, but you know he's been there, it is even more infuriating. How many times have I listened to you rail against the skunks that get into your chicken house? But you don't see 'em."

"I smell 'em," she replied.

That time I had the last word. "Well, my smeller is better than yours. I smell banks." She got the point and laughed.

Emma ran the Fiddleback on an incorruptible cash basis. If a hand needed money for an emergency, she counted it out on the spot or assumed his indebtedness. During one excessively depressed period financially, the crew voluntarily relinquished their wages for eight months. No one starved, including the cattle, and the well-being of the Fiddleback was unimpaired. It was the sort of existence Karl Marx had in mind when he envisioned a social order constructed on the principle "from each according to his ability to each according to his needs," a society in which the "state" as he and Engels defined it, had "withered away." The Fiddleback, however, was not modelled on a theory. The state had not withered away. It had never come into existence - or even a microcosmic replica thereof. Now that we are cursed with it, how do we get rid of it? Or trim its claws and remove its fangs as the framers of the Constitution attempted to do. To indulge further in a little horseplay with Plato, the beast has been let loose from the pit, the problem is putting it back. Marx was a rationalist with an erroneous disbelief in the doctrine of original sin. As Jean Daniels would have said of him, "He had a brand new deck, but it was shy the joker."

iii

Specifically, what triggered my manic compulsion for "explanation" and, consequently, this convoluted appendix, were some benevolent criticisms levelled against technical aspects of my contributions to literature on the cowboy as they appeared in previous articles. I am never annoyed by well-founded criticism, I am only disgusted with myself for getting tangled in my own rope. Invalid criticism, however, is disturbing if you are seriously concerned with establishing a point. It clouds the trail. I may be able to cut back some of the dust-raising *cimmarones* before they slip in and rile the herd.

For example, objections have been raised against my inconsistencies in cowboy vocabulary, diction, dialect and pronunciation. The answer is that cowboys themselves were inconsistent. First off, almost every one of them born since 1890 had better than the equivalent of what is today called "secondary education." They were capable of speaking correct english if they wished and whenever the occasion required it. They were incontestably more eloquent and articulate than the majority of the students I encountered in college teaching since the second world war. An important linguistic trait in which cowboys were consistent is that they never used jargon. When actively engaged in working cattle, however, a *patois* of their own developed that was consistently inconsistent. This was especially evident in the sphere of double, and even triple, negatives and in leaving off the g's in present participles. Sometimes it was done, sometimes it warn't. There are always subtle matters of euphony, harmony, context and deliberate dissonance to be taken into account. Most important is irony and the "put-on." Whenever someone comes across with flawless consistency in stock rustic dialect, the speaker is either a "cotton-pickin' lint-back" or a phony. Reproduced by Alfred Henry Lewis, it is caricature. The cowboy was no lint-back and he did not hail from Wolfville or Dogpatch.

Pat Fee, who was born and raised among cowhands, savvies all this, but she was bothered by what she regarded as my personal atrocities. "Sometimes," she objected, "you have yourself talking like a cowhand and sometimes like yourself." She could have answered this objection herself, but what was actually disturbing her was the unpleasant thought that a trusted friend was writing like a fake. Pat first made my acquaintance in an intellectual environment and not until several years later was she exposed to my experiences as a cowhand. On the other hand, Peter Watts, a distinguished language scholar and author of *A Dictionary of the Old West* whose contact with me was as a cowhand who had broken into print rather than as a professor of history, had this to say: "A man has two languages - the one he is forced to use every day in the city and his heart language, the one he is most comfortable with. Owen Ulph partly thinks in dialect, even though his every day speech may be more general American." The thought of speaking "general American" is worse than comparing my priceless prose to "the pungency of a goat shed during a warm rain."

Well - take your choice. Personally, I ain't got no heart, but I sure as hell make a lot of use of my think-tank even if what comes out never seems to have much effect on my behavior. Speech is a habit and a contagious one. When engrossed in line-camp conversation I spoke like myself (whoever that is) until the mood of the discussion wrung the poetic vigor of the vernacular from my throat. Also, when working cattle, a language with hair on it grabbed the reins. "Goddammit, Henry, kick that muley sonovabitch out of here and if that fucking Tiger won't get in gear, rack his fucking ass!"

To speak moderately, "Excuse me, Henry, my

friend, but would you be so considerate as to remove that obtuse hornless cow from the vicinity of the corral. She's interfering seriously with our efforts to cut these other cattle. If Tiger persists in his sluggish attitude, I strongly recommend that you apply your romal to his rump in a sufficiently rigorous manner to convince him that he should respond with greater alacrity."

Both modes of address were available to me, but I suggest that the second would have been the put-on and the first natural. On certain occasions the second alternative could be employed as a form of self-mimicry that, if one's timing were astute, would always be good for a laugh and would ignite a conflagration of competitive wit. In the heat, dust and bedlam of corral work, however, no one would have had the time to listen to such elegance of expression, let along decode it.

As far as transmitting dialect to the written page through bizarre spelling is concerned, I have tried to adhere to the principle of retaining standard spelling as long as the pronunciation is not significantly altered thereby. Moreover, as I write I am practicing my own brand of Speak-Memory. These former saddle cronies are here with me and I write as I hear them talk. They are not embellished. They may be portrayed in a more picturesque fashion than they performed in actuality, not because I exaggerate, but because much of the fungus of daily routine has been eliminated so that the essence of their actions and personalities emerges vividly and clearly. I do not subscribe to the school of realism that requires characters to comb their hair, brush their teeth, button their shirts, make trips to the bathroom and act out all the trivia of daily existence. These activities only constitute legitimate subject matter for a writer if they are essential to reconstructing a scene significant to the action, characterization or the point of the narrative. Otherwise such guff should be thrown to the magpies. I do not represent this production as perfection. I believe its sins to be those of omission rather than commission and I am not strewing it with booby-traps to discombobulate expected critics. I'm only warning the potential nit-pickers to pick at their own risk. They may latch onto some nits that will be plumb elated to find fresh feeding grounds.

This brings us over the crest of a ridge from which we can drop back down to base camp and finish covering the dog - either with an old saddle blanket to keep the flies, the rain or the snow off him while he grabs some shut-eye, or with a few shovels-full of sand to discourage the crows and coyotes as we plant him for keeps. If Jean's version of the origin of this odd phrase were accepted as gospel, it would not be a fitting caption for this appendix. It rings too much like a death knell - empty saddles in the old corral - an epitaph fading from one of the sun-baked head-boards on the barren slope at the mouth of Ophir Canyon. And I'm far from finished with either the Fiddleback or the subject of cowboys. I'm figuring on three more attempts at masterpieces of verbal sculpture before someone shuts the gate. Barney Manor contended that we all "argufied" the matter too much. "That there sayin' just come frum building the dog house." Barney would bleat like an old ewe when he talked. "Everybody whoever homesteaded this country brung a dog with 'em. After they throwed up the barn, some sheds and a shack fer themselves, they'd finally get around to the dog. After old Bowser had his hut, they'd figure they was settled down fer the winter."

True or not, Barney's testimony has two or three points in its favor. It rescues Ed Fisher's figure of speech from the despised sheepmen and squares with the fact that Ed never used the expression at the end of the spring round-up, but only after the fall gather which often ran into late November with winter already having sent out a couple of advance notices. When Ed said, "Well, that about covers the dog," we knew it was time to roll our cotton and head back for the home ranch where we would "sleep soft," sit on chairs at a table and eat from plates we didn't have to wash ourselves. It also carried promise of the greatest luxury of all - a three-hour bull-session in Darrough's big pool at the hot-springs soaking stratified layers of dirt from our grime-stiffened hides. People who bathe regularly miss the euphoric joy of feeling clean - even if the feeling doesn't last very long.

On the other hand, there wasn't one of us whose innards didn't waver when fall round-up was over. It was the apex of the cow-puncher's year. Much of the time was spent in the high country where we drank clear, cold "sweetwater," where a smooth silken breeze swept lightly from the thinly wooded hills setting the clusters of aspen to shimmering and freshening every afternoon. Nights were always cool.

Sleep was a pleasant, dream-free coma that eased the aches and stiffness from the body. Appetities were keen and the simplest pleasures were given a fine edge by the life of severe contrasts. Riding was rigorous and tough. Casualties among men and horses were frequent. Some member of the crew was always crippled up, but seldom enough to require hospitalization or medical attention beyond Ed or Jean's rough-hewn but effective first aid. In fact, cowhands seldom saw the inside of a hospital. If they were injured too badly to climb into the saddle, they were usually dead. The word "usually" makes room for those exceptions listed under the rubric, "stove-up."

While gruelling, the work of the fall round-up was challenging, a substantial part of it being conducted individually or in pairs. It toned up one's initiative. It was creative and produced a sense of physical and psychological buoyancy for which the term "exhilarating" was coined. It was a state of mind far from conducive to the vulgar beligerency on which hackneyed "westerns" depend. On the contrary, it was an existence capped by consummate companionship and friendship, not only with the men riding with you, but with your string. One may sing the praises of the short horse, the night horse, the roper, the whittler or the hot-blood, but the circle horse that sticks with you through the animating ordeals of the round-up is the true cow-horse whose magnetic equinality penetrates the barrier between man and animal. My apprehensiveness with regard to all the horse-struck people I have known is that their attitude is one of *users*. They love to *own* horses, groom them, adorn them, pamper them, show them, exhibit their ribbons and display trophies and statuettes in their living rooms, and ride them on treated turf, but it is only among cowhands that I have witnessed what I can call genuine respect, appreciation, concern and affection for the horse. (Here I go, alienating another sect of potential consumers!) Jean Daniels accompanied me to a horse-show one time. We had to drive over two hundred miles to Vegas to get there, but that wasn't what bothered us. He was just reluctant to go along and gave no sign of succumbing to my pressures until I said, "Damn it, Jean, I don't want to go either, but I have these two fucking tickets Floyd Lamb give me. They're box seats and suckers are paying two-fifty a-piece for 'em and I don't want to waste 'em." There was no one I have every known more *absolutely indifferent* to money than Jean and my argument was pretty stupid. But it was the word "waste" that got through to him. We must have shared a similar genetic code. Anyway - we went. By now you've probably assayed Jean out as ninety percent misanthrope (and me about the same) so our opinions probably won't pack much weight. Admittedly, Jean was no sentimentalist. Neither am I and it was reassuring for me to discover, as we watched ornate specimens of equine symmetry and elegance canter around the oiled arena, that he shared my viewpoint.

"I'll stick with old Whitey," he said as we left the stadium.

There is no way to describe effectively for readers what the fall round-up, or any part of cowpunching for that matter, was "like." The only solution is to take him (or her) along - as I aim to do in *The Leather Throne* for which this entire profile of the Fiddleback and its crew is primarily an extended preface. Although "covering the dog" implies some sort of conclusion to something regardless of what interpretation of the phrase one adopts, and since the major task of restoring cowboys to their true stature and giving them the kind of credit they actually deserve is still before us, the metaphor could be considered inappropriate at this stage of the drive. Nevertheless, the heavy brush country is behind us and should leave us free and open range for future foraging. The explaining is over! In the next deal, if the deck has to be shuffled and cut at all, it will be cut plumb shallow. The dilemma produced by my quixotic desire to allow the actors and the events to speak on their own behalf, and my irrepressible urges to intervene as a dude wrangler, scout for the wagon train, and general interpreter will have been resolved. You have been introduced to the central characters and exposed to enough of their deportment to know whether you will want any more to do with them. Furthermore, you have been subjected to me at my worst and are enough acquainted with my background and asserted motives not to have to ask, as did a reader of a preliminary draft of *The Leather Throne*, "Who is the narrator? His role is unclear. Why is he in the story at all?"

It occurred to me that any person who asked these questions wouldn't be able to find his bridle if it was hanging around his neck. The narrator was *me* and he was there to tell the story fer chrissakes! He wasn't meant to be anything but a detached observer. He had to participate in the action now and then to justify his wages so I used him to open and shut gates.

Anyway, the fact that these questions were raised discouraged me from counting on much sagacity from readers. It should be pointed out that this feller was a professor of literature with a Ph.D. from Harvard and the "role" of such scholars is to *ask* questions not to be able to *answer* them. However, when I informed him that the role of the narrator was the same as that of Chaucer in *The Canterbury Tales* and he responded with a blank stare, I felt mildly frustrated. "Goddammit, Sam," I almost spluttered after an interval of silence, "*I* was there!"

"When were you at Canterbury?" he asked.

Ed Fisher is my nemesis. I can hear his dry voice distinctly. "Now that you've tipped your hole-card, why are you continuing to play out your hand."

This time I had the answer. "I could have three more of 'em under cover."

"Oh," he said quietly. . . "I didn't realize you were playing solitaire."

If there are further questions, consult the glossary. Class dismissed.

a Working Vocabulary

Discretely selected from the *Fiddleback Almanac*

Apple horn:

The name is self-descriptive. It refers to the type of horn most easily strangled when, gripped by terror, the rider is anticipating being dislodged. It is also excellent for impaling its victims through the navel should the horse decide to take a back-flip. The apple horn has advantages over the flat-top "hot-cake horn." It also has disadvantages. Henry and Zane were unimpeachable authorities. Zane used an apple horn. Henry swore by the flat-top which is called a "dinner plate."

Bangtails:

Mustang or wild horse mares, but not necessarily limited to that sex. Once upon a time an uncombed tail was the sign of an unbroken horse, but the custom tended to die out.

Beef-cut:

When "parting-out," the steers destined for the feed lots were usually designated as "the beef-cut."

Bible:

The small folder of cigaret papers, so called for their similarity in weight and texture to the pages of old fashioned bibles and prayer-books - except that the cigaret papers were pale brown in color. The little cloth bags of *Bull Durham* were equipped with a packet of Wheat Straw papers, and a string with a cardboard tab at one end about the size of a wooden nickel - excellent for holding between the teeth while building a smoke and hanging out of the vest pocket like a fob the rest of the time. In those days the "Marlboro Man" was a polished young fellow in tails or a tuxedo who poised his "tailor-made" in a conspicuous holder. Later, he changed his clothes and threw away the holder. He also acquired a taste for "horseback riding."

Book-wrangler

A term of derision, but not directed against cowboys addicted to reading. It referred to individuals whose relationship with cows was confined to an office desk. Except for a brief period when B.A. Sweet swept the ranch with a cyclone of efficiency and swept out again humbled, but no wiser, the Fiddleback was spared the luxury of clerical assistance. To the cowhand, "statistics" was a synonym for "fairy-tales." Cattle counts were conducted from the back of a horse with a pocket-knife and a willow stick or a piece of easily knotted cord. Ed Fisher relied on the precision of his eyes and memory. One of Jean Daniel's copious recollections began: "Reminds me of the time up at the old Y-Bench when that there banker feller from Reno dropped his fountain-pen in the dirt and while he was climbing down to get it forty odd head romped through the gate. He got flustered and dropped his tally-book. His horse fiddle-foots around because that banker is making him nervous, steps on his pen and pisses on all his figures. . ." Amen!

Carving horse:

An undignified name for a cutting horse - sometimes called a "whittler" or a "cleaver." Other names worthy of Jack-the-Ripper were occasionally applied. Henry would brag that his horse, Kewpie, "could cut a ground-squirrel away from its own shadow," to which Zane would reply,

"That pampered, sugar-fed frump couldn't cut a porcupine toward water if it was on a sand-bar and dying of thirst."

Cold-storage box:

Accommodations at the morgue or the cemetary. Jean Daniels, in addition to being a top-cowhand, was a jack-of-all-trades. His talent as a carpenter had somewhere along the line suckered him into nailing together a coffin for Tsar Nicholas II who, contrary to popular belief, was not shot in a cellar at Ekaterinburg in 1918, but escaped through Siberia and died in Austin, Nevada in the mid-thirties. Thenceforth, the last request of everyone who died in Austin and vicinity was to be buried in a Daniels' Casket. Jean was not kept too busy. The death rate in Austin was low and the climate, dry in summer and sub-zero in winter, preserved bodies well. During the time I knew Jean, he was seldom required to make more than one or two boxes a year - except once, and that story will be recounted at a more appropriate time.

Cow-chips:

The cowhand's barbecue briquets.

Coyotin' round the rim:

Sniffing around. Casing the situation. Looking over the edge. Is it worth the risk? Did Emma or Wiggins forget to shut the door to the chicken shed? How much can I get away with? Play it sly.

Campfire conversation with Association Rules ignored.

Dog-hole:

This is not a depression dug by a dog to lie down in or in which to bury a bone. It is the entrance to a prairie-dog's home. Several of them make up a "dog-town." Badgers will enlarge them in their eagerness to savor the delicacy of a "family dinner." The badger is of value in eradicating a nuisance, but his own talents at excavation might be considered a cure that is worse than the disease. A badger hole, although it can be seen more easily, is a greater threat to a horse in a high run than a dog-hole. On the range, one is always faced with the problem of choosing between evils and there is seldom such a thing as a "lesser evil." Life is like looking at a menu at drive-in restaurants.

Doughgods:

Baking powder biscuits made by such skilled craftsmen as Jean Daniels and Jack Chatovitch. Whenever the term "biscuit" was used it referred to a saddle horn. Contrariwise, if biscuits were like adobe (raw or baked) they were called "saddlehorns."

Drift rights:

The "right" to run cows on the public lands is legally regarded as a form of property. One of the more commendable traits of cattle is that they seem to lack what humans speciously call "the property instinct." On open, unfenced range cows fail to show proper respect for John Locke's "inalienable right" and graze where they please. Their owners, consequently, have "drift rights" on neighboring range. Their riders, however, are expected to put forth a reasonable effort to see that the owners' cattle keep their vagrant habits to a minimum. Negligence, however, in the performance of this duty is not unknown.

Equinality:

A word of my own coinage designed to endow the horse with the individuality that the term "personality" does for human beings. I did not want to insult the horse by referring to its personality. The British gentry - great horse-lovers (Cromwell) and, therefore, great statesmen - would address close, respected friends as "old horse." It was a colloquialism conveying affection, admiration, peerage. In short, it was highly complimentary. Readers who manage to stick with me should come to understand *why*. The substitution of the machine for the horse was one of the great cultural disasters in the history of civilized life. I am not arguing in favor of machine-wrecking (Luddite Riots and *Erewhon*), but for intelligent direction and control. The machine should have been used to relieve horses (and men) from abominable exploitation, but should never have displaced genteel transportation (the way golf-mobiles have displaced caddies). Until society places quality of life above vulgar acquisition, accumulation and lust for sensual gratification and indolence, the progress of civilization will not only be retarded, it will regress to a new Stone Age that will be infinitely worse than the old one. Historical evidence indicating that the Cro-magnon was probably the most superior specimen of *homo-sapiens* evolution ever produced has not been confuted.

Heifer Drive:

This is not the name of an avenue passing between a row of sorority houses although it has often been used as such. It refers to the occasion on which me and Holly drove 200 head of these unruly critters from the Home Ranch to the range at Millers - only to have them back-trail during the night. The episode is referred to twice and there is a superficial discrepancy. In one version, the drive occupied 5 days and the other 3. The conflicting statistics are disturbing in so far as they are related to the perverse return trek of the cattle. The distance from the Home Ranch to Millers was over a hundred miles and consumed five days. In the course of the drive we passed through Diamond Hook ranch - which was now owned by the Fiddleback and was roughly halfway between the Home Ranch and the winter pasture. When Holly and I left the herd, we drove the stock truck, loaded with our horses, directly through the desert instead of routing ourselves through Tonopah by way of the paved highway.

We stopped that night at the Diamond Hook where Jean Daniels was shacking out. This is where the cattle showed up the following morning and a big hunk of the drive had to be done over again. The horses, who understood the whole situation, were more pissed off than we were and demonstrated their vexation with those damned heifers in the vengeful way they harried them back. Once again, I must remind readers of Henry's insistence upon patience on the part of his audience.

Hired Man on Horseback:

A poem famous among *afficionados* of the range by Eugene Manlove Rhodes, a well-known western writer of the twenties who, while deploring the cult of the cowboy as gunslinger, was equally nettled by reference to his fellows as "simply riding farmhands." Rhodes' heroes are "knights errant," dangerously close to being cute and seldom encounter cows during their quaint adventures. Nevertheless, they are genuine cowboy types. Rhodes' major works have been recently re-issued by the University of Oklahoma Press, featuring lively introductions by W.H. Hutchinson. Rhodes' tales were written when the air was pure, the water was pure and the women purer still. Well. . . use your own judgement. . .

Hollow-horn:

A catch-all term to describe any physical or mental affliction of animal or man that defies conventional classification and for which there is no known remedy other than drilling a hole into the horn, filling it with sand and plugging it. "If this don't work, just knock it on the head." It is a disease prevalent among public officials.

Hooley-ann and Hoolihan:

These terms are often confused. The only thing they have in common is that both are head-catches. The former is a roping term that describes a large, flat loop. It appeals to amateurs, but if not done properly, it becomes a "Mother Hubbard." The latter is a macho, rodeo *stunt* performed by doubles for John Wayne, *et. al.* No rope is used. Bulk is a great asset in hoolihaning and, ideally, the acrobat should outweigh the steer. This was hard on horses packing the hoolihaners and was banned from rodeo. It is about to be re-introduced, however, substituting a helicopter for the horse.

Hot-rod:

An electrically charged poking tube used to prod cattle between the rails of loading chutes and runways to inspire them to move with enthusiasm. A similar device was to "high-life" them. This consisted of squirting a chemical compound on them that evaporated so rapdily it created the sensation of a branding iron. Ranch children (on outfits that tolerated the presence of these little savages) loved to use it on dogs and cats and, less unmercifully, on each other.

Jamoka:

Coffee. The term is of disputed origin. Some hold it to be a pun fabricated by combining mocha with Jamaica. Others argue that it combines mocha with jam which was used in place of sugar as a sweetener. This crude habit never invaded the Fiddleback, however, where coffee was either drunk black or poured into the sugar bowl and eaten with a spoon. For this reason, Wiggins devised a cruet like an over-sized salt shaker from which the sugar could be vigorously shaken *out*, but coffee could not be poured *in*.

Jerk-line:

A teamsters' long rein for controlling the lead mules.

Judas steer:

A decoy used to dupe the herd into following him into some sort of unpleasant adventure like a branding corral, a loading chute or the vestibule of the slaughter-house. It is one of the most far-reaching and significant of cowboy customs, having been introduced into our political system by which nominees for public office seduce the urban herd call, "voters."

Leppy:

An orphaned calf. Leppies were easily identified by their pot bellies. They have been called "four-legged bon-bons," and compared to tadpoles that got hung up trying to turn themselves into frogs.

Light a shuck:

To depart without unnecessary ceremony. As Emma Rogers remarked of a hand who had left the Fiddleback before sun-up. "He didn't take time to come and collect his wages."

"I saw him go," Henry said. "He lit out so fast he'd rid a mile before his horse could get under him."

The origin of the expression dates back to a time when corn husks were bound into makeshift torches and used as lamps to get from the wagon to where one's horse was staked. The shucks are gone but "lighting out" remains.

Long ear:

A calf without an ear-mark. Usually one that had reached an age when it should have been branded. A long-ear was a temptation to the greed of Grand Aquisitors.

Medicine-tongued:

A smooth talker. Slick. Not a commendable trait. It implies deceit. Cowhands are far from silent and it is not "talking" that is deplored, but the use of a rash of words as a dust storm to hide one's thoughts. Jean, as usual, expressed the sentiment succinctly when he remarked about a particular Nevada politician, "When that feller begins to talk I get to feelin' my pocket's bein' picked."

Mrs. Gummidge:

This dowdy old housekeeper always described

herself as "a poor lorn cretur." Some eastern magazine editors who rejected the manuscript of "The Cowboss" regarded the reference to her as "too arcane" in an article about cowboys. Mrs. Gummidge was condemned to serve time between the covers of Dickens' *David Copperfield,* a tedious book that every high-school kid who suffered through an English class before 1929 had to read. Amidst that cast of bores, it is no wonder that Mrs. Gummidge felt sorry for herself. Anyway, a copy of Dickens' labored tome could be found on the Fiddleback bookshelves along with a gallery of musty classics including *St. Elmo, The Scarlet Pimpernel, Plutarch's Lives,* Henry Herbert Knibbs' *Riding Kid from Powder River,* all the works of Jack London and Rex Beach and a set of Thomas Babington Macaulay's *History of England.* There was also a *Bible* in mint condition under several layers of dust. No Fiddleback puncher would have thought of Ed Fisher's name for the old lop-horned cow as arcane - even had they known the meaning of the word.

Navvy:

The most decrepit horse conceivable. The allusion is to animals owned by the Navajos. It is not intended as a reflection on the Indians. The poor condition of their stock was usually due to the fact that both the horse and its owner were existing on the fringe of starvation.

Night rider:

This could be any hand on night herding duty. In times past it was used to refer to anyone "on the dodge." Night herding died out with fenced pastures and stock-trucks. There were some circumstances when it was still practical at the Fiddleback. We had one fellow for a short time who was particularly good at it and who we called, "Owl-Eyes." Naturally, there was much irreverent speculation on how he had developed this rare faculty. Jean delivered the accepted verdict. "Owl-Eyes don't see no better in the dark than nobody else. He's just a feller that don't care to be seen and don't want to see nobody."

Riding the river:

This has become a stock macho phrase in hack westerns. "He's a good man to ride the river with." It supposedly denotes every masculine, heroic virtue. As a matter of fact, the phrase was first coined to describe the calibre of a horse - not a man. In days of the old trail drives, swimming rivers at flood stage was probably the most hazardous of all a trail rider's labors - and the dependable river horse was his margin between life and death. "That's a horse you can ride the river with" was the highest praise you could bestow upon the noble beast. All coinage is ultimately debased. When the phrase began to be applied to men, it began to lose the purity of its meaning. In western fiction it is loosely used to elevate any rough-housing hooligan to heroic stature - regrettably. But it is, nevertheless, consoling to reflect upon the fact that the highest compliment one can pay a man is to compare him to a horse!

Rusties:

Inferior cattle from leppies to lump-jaws. Davy Stevens, proprietor of the Diamond Hook, collected them. Davy should have been heading up the Department of Health, Education and Welfare. (An interesting example of Bureaucratic Euphemisms, is it not? One is continually reminded of Orwell's Ministry of Plenty, Ministry of Peace and Ministry of Truth!)

Scours:

An intestinal disorder afflicting calves, young colts and cowhands who drank Reese River water after Bastille Day at an altitude below 10,000 feet.

Seven deadly sins:

Pride, covetousness, lust, anger, gluttony, envy and sloth. My contention was that Ed Fisher and all good cowhands were completely immune to five of them and the two of which they could be accused - pride and anger - when indulged by them were actually cardinal virtues. The world does need recreating. God did a sloppy job. Sometimes Wiggins would sub for him and after a few foul-ups, Zane, whose short fuse could attain the proportions of a sin, would shout at him, "Shit, man, if you don't know what you're doing, get the hell out of the corral!"

Shirt-rats:

Lice. Also called "cooties" and several other unsavory epithets best rated X to the nth power.

Take (your, his, her, my) turns:

This refers to dallying - in which the rope is wrapped rapidly counter-clockwise around the horn after the roper has "made his ketch." It is advisable to keep one's fingers away from the neck of the horn unless one wants them amputated. The maneuver is unnecessary if one "ties hard-and-fast." The relative merits of the two systems will be a subject of controversy until air-conditioning is installed in hell. Like many such arguments, it grows more heated as the issue becomes more irrelevant. The old-timers didn't care much one way or the other. It was just another aspect of the day's work and they could usually rope either way, adapting their methods to circumstance.

Talking turkey:

Laying it on the line.

Tree:

The wooden frame of a saddle. The term was commonly adopted as a name for a full contraption - like *hull, trap, rig,* and many others.

Twitch:

A diabolical device for taking the horse-play out of a misguided horse suffering from the delusion that it possessed "rights." A loop is placed around the animal's upper lip, tightened like a garotte and held fast with a stick. The treatment brought results and there were times when one might be driven to such a degree of exasperation and loss of patience as to feel justified in using it, but it was a treatment too easily abused by thugs. Twitches, like hand-guns and switch-blades, could be purchased ready-made. This is not a devious argument for gun-control, just a gentle reminder that the root of all evil lies in the individual. It is what the world needs today!